Contents

I AM NOT ASHAMED

50 Devotions For Teens on Romans

by

Laurie Polich

DIMENSIONS
FOR LIVING
NASHVILLE

I AM NOT ASHAMED:
50 DEVOTIONS FOR TEENS ON ROMANS

This book is printed on acid-free, recycled paper.

ISBN 0687-08118-1

Cover design: Kelly Chinn

03 04 05 06 07 08 09 10 11 12—10 9 8 7 6 5 4 3 2 1

MANUFACTURED IN THE UNITED STATES OF AMERICA

Dedication

To Brian,

Who gently moved me to face my fears

And helped me not be ashamed.

Acknowledgments

Special thanks to:

Earl Palmer, for shedding tremendous insight into this great book;

Judy Polich Coe, for being my mom—and a huge cheerleader
in my life;

Ramona Hockett, putting her life in God's hands
and making her "mom" proud;

Brian, Isaac, and Rosie Tucker, for teaching me a new dimension
of love and grace.

Introduction

Are you ready to have your life changed? That's what the book of Romans tends to do. Martin Luther read the book of Romans and started the Reformation. That was the movement that gave birth to the Protestant church. Augustine read the book of Romans and became known as Saint Augustine. He was one of the most loved and respected church fathers the world has ever known. Karl Barth read the book of Romans and influenced some of the world's greatest Christians. His Barman Declaration led German Christians (including Dietrich Bonheoffer) to start an uprising against Hitler's regime. So the question is, What will the book of Romans do to you?

Before you get started, there are a few things you should know about this devotional. It's purpose is to guide you through the book of Romans. At the top of each page, you'll find the Scripture reference that pertains to each devotion. After that, you'll see several of the verses written out. You could read only these verses and still get something out of the devotional; however, to get the most out of your study time, you should first read the entire passage from your Bible. As much as I want you to read my book, it's *that* book that will change you. I just hope to provide some added insight along the way.

Questions after each devotional will help you process what you're reading and discover how Paul's words can speak to your own life. That's the miracle of God's Word—although you're reading words addressed to the Christians in Rome, the words have the power to touch you. As you open yourself up to each passage, you'll find that God will speak to you. So take some time to reflect on the questions. It will make your time with God even richer.

Finally, let me say, on a personal note, that this was the most difficult book I've ever written. It was also the most rewarding. The book of Romans is rich and deep, complex and difficult—and I spent many hours staring at my computer screen, wondering how to make sense of it for you. But it was worth the effort. Writing this book had a deep effect on my life. My prayer is that reading this book—and more importantly Paul's book—will have the same effect on you.

Will You Take the Call?

Romans 1:1-10

Paul, a servant of Christ Jesus, called to be an apostle and set apart for the gospel of God—the gospel he promised beforehand through his prophets in the Holy Scriptures regarding his Son, who as to his human nature was a descendant of David, and who through the Spirit of holiness was declared with power to be the Son of God by his resurrection from the dead: Jesus Christ our Lord. Through him and for his name's sake, we received grace and apostleship to call people from among all the Gentiles to the obedience that comes from faith. And you also are among those who are called to belong to Jesus Christ. (Romans 1:1-6, NIV)

...Not Ashamed of the Gospel

If you've ever made a collect call, you know that the experience can leave you hanging. The operator announces your name to the person who picks up the phone, and asks whether he or she will accept the charges. If the person on the other end says no, your call is promptly disconnected. (This is a bad sign if you're calling your parents.) But the person who answers the phone has to accept the charges in order for the call to go through.

In the opening passage of Romans, Paul says that he was "called to be an apostle and set apart for the gospel of God" (verse 1). Paul's call was a little bit like a collect call; because at some point, he had to decide whether or not he would accept the charges. Paul's description of himself as a servant of Christ shows that he not only accepted

his call, he embraced it—and this says something about Paul's trust in God. Unlike a collect call, this call from God didn't just cost him money—it cost him his life. Now that's an expensive call!

Many people think that being a Christian

...Not Ashamed of Digging Deeper

means asking God to join you as you live the life you want to live. But in reality, being a Christian means asking God to direct you as you live the life God wants you to live. That's how Paul understood his life when he accepted God's call. The Book of Romans shows us how Paul answered God's call, because we witness Paul's commitment in every passage.

But the call of God is not extended only to Paul. Paul says that God extends the same call to any Gentiles who are willing to receive it (verses 5-6). That means God has sent out a collect call for you and me as well. But remember, if you accept the call, there is only one way to pay the charges—by giving God your life.

Will you take the call?

1. What do you think it means to be "set apart for the gospel of God?"

...Not Ashamed of Living for Christ

Do you think that this applies only to Paul or to all Christians?

2. In verse 5, Paul says he is calling people to the "obedience that comes from faith." What does that mean?

3. How much do you show your faith through your obedience to God?

In what areas of your life do you need more faith? In what areas of your life do you need more obedience?

I Am not Ashamed

Romans 1:11-17

I am not ashamed of the gospel, because it is the power of God for the salvation of everyone who believes: first for the Jew, then for the Gentile. For in the gospel a righteousness from God is revealed, a righteousness that is by faith from first to last, just as it is written: "The righteous will live by faith." (Romans 1:16-17, NIV)

...Not Ashamed of the Gospel

Where were you on September 11, 2001? Most likely you remember because of the horrible events of that day. Four planes were hijacked; and three of them were flown into crowded buildings, killing thousands of people in an instant. Hearing that it all happened in the name of religion made the events of that sad day even worse.

Many Moslems disassociated themselves from the hijackers, saying that their acts of violence did not accurately represent Islam. I can only imagine the shame many Moslems experienced as the terrorists praised their god for the "victory" they achieved. It wasn't exactly the kind of witness that draws people to faith. In fact it had the opposite effect—most people wanted to be as far away from the terrorists' religion as possible.

Paul's words in this passage speak of a very different faith. He knows that there may be reasons for people to be ashamed of how other people have acted in the name of their beliefs; and he wants to tell us why he is not ashamed of the gospel. First, because the gospel is powerful; it provides salvation for everyone. Second, it is good. It brings righteousness, instead of judgment, which results in life, not death. And finally, it is free. You don't have to earn God's love. All you have to do is believe.

...Not Ashamed of Digging Deeper

If only the hijackers had known this faith. It might have spared us from the shameful way they attempted to earn the approval of a god who doesn't exist. Four hijacked planes. Three horrible attacks. What a shameful day.

Or was it? One plane didn't hit its intended target that day. Instead, it crashed into a field. A small band of passengers had stormed the cockpit, led in part by a Christian man named Todd Beamer. With the words "Let's roll," these passengers stopped the hijackers, with courage and confidence. Todd was not ashamed to act on his faith, even while facing death. Those passengers died so that others might live.

"Let's roll" may have been the last words Todd said on earth, but they were his first words in heaven. In that moment, we witnessed unashamed faith. Let us never be ashamed.

1. What reasons might people be ashamed for what they believe?

...Not Ashamed of Living for Christ

Have you ever been ashamed of your faith?

2. What reasons does Paul give in verses 16-17 for why we shouldn't be ashamed of the gospel?

Which one stands out most to you? Why?

3. According to verse 17, where does our righteousness come from—us or God? How does that make you feel about your faith?

The Frog in the Kettle

Romans 1:18-32

For the wrath of God is revealed from heaven against all ungodliness and wickedness of those who by their wickedness suppress the truth....For though they knew God, they did not honor him as God or give thanks to him, but they became futile in their thinking, and their senseless minds were darkened....

...Not Ashamed of the Gospel

Therefore God gave them up in the lusts of their hearts to impurity, to the degrading of their bodies among themselves, because they exchanged the truth about God for a lie and worshiped and served the creature rather than the Creator, who is blessed forever! Amen.
(Romans 1:18, 21, 24-25, NRSV)

Have you ever eaten frog legs? If you ever decide to, you'll have to boil the frog first. Here's the way to do it: Put the frog into a pot filled with warm water and slowly heat the water to a boil. You won't even need to put a lid on the pot. The frog will just sit there calmly ready to donate its legs to your fancy meal. BUT DON'T BOIL THE WATER FIRST—otherwise, you'll have a very active game of leapfrog on your kitchen stove.

This is a great analogy for how we fall into sin, and that's what Paul is talking about in this passage. Sin begins in our minds—when we want to do something we know God doesn't want us to do. Eventually, we become so focused on what it is we want that we stop caring what God thinks altogether. And that's when we're headed for trouble.

After enough rationalizing, we sin. It usually starts small; and we feel bad, promising never to do it again. But the temptation becomes greater once the sin has been tried, and we find it harder to stay away. So we stay in the pot, when we should jump out.

...Not Ashamed of Digging Deeper

The funny thing is, sin never delivers the satisfaction it promises. After one sin, we are soon ready for an even bigger sin. And if we keep going, we'll find ourselves joining the boiling frogs.

If you look over the list of sins Paul describes, chances are you'll react with a shudder. The sins seem so extreme you feel you'd never commit them. But if you look closer at the process, you'll see how sin works. It doesn't throw you into a pot of boiling water. It gently lures you into a pot of warm water and slowly boils you to death.

So learn your lesson from a frog. No matter how warm and cozy it feels, sin eventually leads to death. That's why God doesn't want you to do it. God's desire is to give you life.

...Not Ashamed of Living for Christ

1. What is the progression of sin Paul describes in this passage?

Have you ever seen this in people around you?

2. Have you ever experienced the progression of sin in your own life?

Did it begin with your mind (thinking about it) or with your actions (spontaneously deciding to do it)?

3. What steps do you need to take to stop the progression of sin in your life? (Think about the things you read, watch, or talk about.)

Make a list of 3 things you will do this week to focus on God, rather than on sin.

Not Me!

Romans 2:1-11

Therefore you have no excuse, whoever you are, when you judge others; for in passing judgment on another you condemn yourself, because you, the judge, are doing the very same things. You say, "We know that God's judgment on those who do such things is in accordance with truth." Do you imagine, whoever you are, that when you judge those who do such things and yet do them yourself, you will escape the judgment of God? (Romans 2:1-3, NRSV)

...Not Ashamed of the Gospel

Have you ever noticed how much easier it is to point out others' mistakes than it is to admit our own? It's as if we see their faults through a magnifying glass, making everything they do seem bigger. But in this passage, Paul takes that magnifying glass and turns it into a mirror. And he invites us to take a closer look at ourselves.

One of the hardest things about becoming a Christian is admitting that we're sinners. Somehow the word *sinner* seems so degrading; we feel like we're not *that* bad. Immediately our mind conjures up a picture of a real sinner—someone who murders, or commits adultery, or steals—and we compare those sins with the petty little sins we've done. Usually, we come out on top.

But when we look at Paul's list of sins in this passage, we see that being judgmental and unrepentant are at the top of the list. Suddenly, we realize that no matter how many sins we've managed to avoid, there are an equal number of sins we've managed to commit. It's not just other people who have a problem; it's us.

...Not Ashamed of Digging Deeper

Admitting your problem is half the solution, because now you know you need help. Paul says, "There will be anguish and distress for everyone who does evil" (verse 9). That isn't just Adolf Hitler, Osama Bin Laden, or the latest child molester in the news. It's us. Evil includes all sin. So even if we rate higher on the moral scale, we still don't rate high enough. God's judgment upon evil is a crisis that faces us all.

Once we understand our problem, we're ready to hear the solution. And Paul will show us what that is as we continue to read Romans. But in the meantime, when you look at someone else's sin through some kind of glass, make it a mirror. You're less likely to judge when you're looking at yourself.

1. Have you ever felt judged by someone else?

If so, how did it feel?

...Not Ashamed of Living for Christ

2. Do you ever judge other people? (This includes gossip.)

If so, why do you think you do that?

3. What does verse 1 say about what happens when you judge someone?

How can this verse help you be less judgmental of others?

Knowing Right From Wrong

Romans 2:12-16

All who have sinned apart from the law will also perish apart from the law, and all who have sinned under the law will be judged by the law. For it is not the hearers of the law who are righteous in God's sight, but the doers of the law who will be justified. When Gentiles, who do not possess the law, do instinctively what the law requires, these, though not having the law are a law unto themselves. They show that what the law requires is written on their hearts.
(Romans 2:12-15a, NRSV)

...Not Ashamed of the Gospel

When I used to get in trouble, there was one excuse I would try with my parents that never seemed to work. Maybe you've tried it too. The excuse was, "You never told me this was wrong." Unfortunately, I was usually met with the same response. It went something like this: "You should have known without my telling you." I hated hearing those words. But I have to admit, most of the time it was true.

In verse 15, Paul talks about a law that is written in our hearts, and there are two ways we know this law is there. The first is when someone does something wrong to us. When someone steals from us, cheats on us, or lies to us, we don't think to ourselves: "Maybe they didn't know it was wrong." We *know* they know it was wrong.

The second way we know there is a law inside us is the guilt we feel when we do something wrong. Deep inside we all have a conscience; and whether or not we listen to our conscience, it's there. People who ignore their consciences do so for a price; and that price is a lack of peace. That's why the famous saying goes: "Let your conscience be your guide."

...Not Ashamed of Digging Deeper

The problem is that the conscience is not just our guide for doing right; it also shows us how bad we can really be. Crazy thoughts go on deep inside of our hearts that we wouldn't want anyone to know about. Our conscience reveals those things; but it cannot fix our problem. It just leaves us knowing what the problem is.

That's why we need something more powerful than our conscience to fix us. Paul, like a good prosecuting attorney, has a few more points to build his case before he tells us what that is. But I'll give you a hint: it's more loving and forgiving than we could ever deserve.

1. Have you ever felt your conscience?

If so, what did it feel like?

2. In what way is our conscience similar to God's voice?

What does this tell you about the way God created us?

3. How does following your conscience bring you peace?

Do you need more peace in your life? If so, how can you get it?

Jewish Law and Christian Faith

Romans 2:17-27

If you are convinced that you are a guide for the blind, a light for those who are in the dark, an instructor of the foolish, a teacher of infants, because you have in the law the embodiment of knowledge and truth—you, then, who teach others, do you not teach yourself?

You who preach against stealing, do you steal? You who say that people should not commit adultery, do you commit adultery? You who abhor idols, do you rob temples? You who brag about the law, do you dishonor God by breaking the law? (Romans 2:19-23, NIV)

...Not Ashamed of the Gospel

Imagine that you and a friend are out sailing, when your boat suddenly capsizes and you find yourselves dog paddling in the ocean. Your friend turns to you and proudly says, "It's a good thing I know a lot about sailing. Because of my studies, I know that we are exactly 500 miles from shore in shark infested waters, and that our position is due west." After a few more facts detailing your predicament, you would soon be tempted to lose your friend. All of his knowledge would only make your situation worse.

What you need at that moment isn't knowledge about how far you are from shore. You need help getting there. This is a good illustration of what Paul is talking about in this passage. The Jews prided themselves on their knowledge of the Law, because they knew God's standards. But knowing God's standards only made their situation worse. Because they knew the Law, they actually *knew* how far they were from God.

Knowing God's standards doesn't solve the problem of living God's standards. The only one who can help us do that

...Not Ashamed of Digging Deeper

is Jesus Christ. The Jews felt that they had all the help they needed in the Law. But the Law only brought the problem into focus—like your friend's knowledge about sailing did. When you're floating way out in an ocean, you need more than knowledge to get you to shore. You need help. In a sense, that's what Paul is trying to communicate in this passage.

The Law couldn't give the Jews salvation; it was there to

show them their need for salvation. The Jews needed something bigger than the Law to save them. They had the information, but they needed more than that. They needed a life-saving relationship with Jesus Christ.

Knowing that you're 500 miles from shore doesn't bring you any closer to getting there. Start swimming, and you'll find out!

1. What do you think is the purpose of the Law?

...Not Ashamed of Living for Christ

2. In what ways does the Law show us our need for God?

3. What "laws" from God do you have the most trouble keeping? (See Exodus 20 if you don't know them.)

How does this help you lean on God?

A Matter of the Heart

Romans 2:28-3:4

For a person is not a Jew who is one outwardly, nor is true circumcision something external and physical. Rather, a person is a Jew who is one inwardly, and real circumcision is a matter of the heart—it is spiritual and not literal. Such a person receives praise not from others but from God. (Romans 2:28-29, NRSV)

...Not Ashamed of the Gospel

Paul has helped us see that knowing the Law only in our heads doesn't advance our position before God, so now he asks a very important question. Is there any advantage in being a Jew, since Jews have been entrusted with the Word of God?

The Jews are special to God, because the Word of God was given to them. But Paul wants to make it clear that simply having God's Word in their brain is not enough. Faith, not knowledge, is the door to God; and faith is a matter of the heart. So, knowing God's Word isn't as important as living it.

I once heard that sitting in church doesn't make you a Christian anymore than sitting in a garage makes you a car. The same is true with being a Jew. Paul makes it clear that a relationship with God is about who you are on the inside, not who you are on the inside, not on the outside. So being Jewish, just like saying that you're a Christian, doesn't cut it. You have to live what you believe.

Before Jesus came, the Jews defined their relationship with God through the Law. But Paul says that there is now a new way to understand God—through faith.

...Not Ashamed of Digging Deeper

So now Paul asks the question, If some Jews were unfaithful to God's commands, does that mean that God's plan for us is ruined? Then he answers the question himself: "No way!" Keeping God's commands may change us; but it doesn't change God. And no matter what we do or don't do, God's faithfulness never changes. It's there for us all.

There are great advantages to having God's Law; but when God's Law isn't kept, there are bigger advantages to having faith. We are, however, called to live out our faith.

Because our lives, more than our words, show what's really true.

1. What advantages do you see in the Jews' having the Law?

...Not Ashamed of Living for Christ

What disadvantages do you see?

2. What does it mean that faith is a matter of the heart?

3. In what ways have you lived from the heart?

In what ways have you lived for outward appearances?

Justifying Sin

Romans 3:5-8

But if our unrighteousness brings out God's righteousness more clearly, what shall we say? That God is unjust in bringing his wrath on us? (I am using a human argument.) Certainly not! If that were so, how could God judge the world? Someone might argue, "If my falsehood enhances God's truthfulness and so **...Not** *increases his glory, why am I still condemned as a sinner?" Why not say—as we are being* **Ashamed** *slanderously reported as saying and as some* **of the Gospel** *claim that we say—"Let us do evil that good may result"? Their condemnation is deserved. (Romans 3:5-8, NIV)*

When I was in school, one of my favorite assignments was being part of a debate. It usually went something like this: The teacher would introduce a controversial issue and then tell you which side of the issue you were supposed to defend. The irony of this assignment was that you had to study the arguments from both sides so that you were prepared to defend your own position and counteract the opposing arguments. It was a secret strategy teachers used to help you learn the issue. (And it also got them off the hook from having to teach you all of the details.)

Paul approaches his audience in Romans like a good debater. He anticipates the arguments from the opposing side to make his case. We've seen how Paul did that in the last two passages.

Now Paul addresses one last extreme perspective from the opposition, as he asks a question we, too, might be led to ask.

He says, in effect, "If our sin doesn't hinder God's goodness, why shouldn't we just  **...Not Ashamed of Digging Deeper** continue to sin?" Then he takes it even further for dramatic effect: "In fact, if our sin brings out God's goodness even more, why not sin even more?"

By presenting this extreme idea in the form of a question, Paul makes his point without having to say it. That is the mark of a great debater. He knows the availability of God's grace may lead us to the idea of sinning more to get more of it.

The fact that we would come up with this idea shows us how full of sin we really are. No one but a sinner could come up with the excuse to sin more to make God look better. And that is exactly the point Paul is trying to make.

1. What is Paul's main point in this passage?

...Not Ashamed of Living for Christ

How does he make his case?

2. Have you ever used God's grace as a license to sin? If so, how?

3. How does God's grace inspire our obedience?

How can you be more obedient as a response to God's grace?

No One Is Good

Romans 3:9-20

"There is no one righteous, not even one; there is no one who understands, no one who seeks God. All have turned away, they have together become worthless; there is no one who does good, not even one. Their throats are open graves; their tongues practice deceit. The poison of vipers is on their lips." ...

...Not Ashamed of the Gospel

Therefore no one will be declared righteous in his sight by observing the law; rather, through the law we become conscious of sin.
(Romans 3:10b-13, 20, NIV)

The nursery rhyme "Humpty Dumpty" seems innocent, but it's really a terrible tale. Think about it:

> Humpty Dumpty sat on a wall.
> Humpty Dumpty had a great fall.
> All the king's horses and all the king's men
> Couldn't put Humpty together again.

The next time you read that rhyme to a kid, you may want to think again. It is not a happy story. It's a sad story, told in a happy sort of way. Paul uses that same tactic in this passage.

In this section of Romans, Paul is continuing to deliver some bad news. But he uses poetry and Scripture to do it. Normally, when people write Scripture to one another, they quote their favorite verses. Paul communicates his message by quoting some "unfavorite" verses, and this makes his point even more profound.

Paul wants to make it clear that we are all sinners—Jews and Gentiles alike. No one can stand blameless before God. Jews are in the same boat as the Gentiles in their standing before God. Paul knows that the Jews won't accept this unless they hear it from a reliable source, so he uses Old Testament verses to make his case. The verses Paul uses are grim and despairing; and the Jews can't argue with him, because the quotes come right from their Scriptures. But the verses speak not only to the Jews; they

...Not Ashamed of Digging Deeper

contain some very bad news for us all.

We are all in trouble, and we need help to save us from our sin. In a sense, we're like Humpty Dumpty. We're fallen people, and we need more than the king's horses and the king's men to put us back together. What we need is the King himself.

1. What indications do you see in the world that people are capable of evil?

...Not Ashamed of Living for Christ

2. What do you see inside yourself that tells you that you are capable of evil?

3. How does God work to steer you away from evil toward good?

How much do you allow this power to work in your life?

The Savior We All Need

Romans 3:21-31

But now a righteousness from God, apart from law, has been made known, to which the Law and the Prophets testify. This righteousness from God comes through faith in Jesus Christ to all who believe. There is no difference, for all have sinned and fall short of the glory of God, and are justified freely by his grace through the redemption that came by Christ Jesus. (Romans 3:21-24, NIV)

...Not Ashamed of the Gospel

In the first three chapters of Romans, Paul has made it clear that we are all in crisis—a crisis we can't fix by ourselves. The distance between our sin and God's holiness is too great; and no matter how good we try to be, we can't be good enough to get there. The Jews thought that they were good enough, because they had God's Law. But they showed more love for keeping God's Law than for God, and their failure put them in the same boat as the rest of us.

One way to illustrate this is to imagine being on a boat off the West coast, with the Olympic swim team. If all of you decided to jump off the boat and swim to Hawaii, you would probably not make it as far as the Olympic swimmers; but none of you would make it all the way. The distance is too great. Eventually, you would all need a lifeboat.

That's what Paul is trying to say in this passage. The Jews may be farther along than the Gentiles in their pursuit of holiness, but nobody is close enough to get to God. So here is the surprising news: God has come to us. By sending Jesus to die on a cross, God gave us the lifeboat we need to get us home. Jesus is not just the Savior some of us need; he's the Savior we all need, because he provides the only way for us to get to God.

...Not Ashamed of Diggin Deeper

All of us have sinned and fall short of the glory of God. But now Paul gives us the good news: We are justified freely by God's grace. It's as if Paul has given us our sentence of death, and now stuns the courtroom by announcing that God will be serving our sentence for us. We haven't earned this gift. All we need to do is decide whether we will receive it.

To put it another way, when a lifeboat comes beside you as you are swimming toward Hawaii, you can still choose whether to get in the boat. But the consequences make it pretty obvious what the best choice is.

1. Why do we need a righteousness apart from the law? (verse 21)

...Not Ashamed of Living for Christ

Who is in need of that righteousness?

2. Is faith more about our work or God's work?

Why?

3. Is your faith more dependent on God or yourself?

In what areas do you need to depend more on God?

Righteousness by Faith

Romans 4:1-12

What then are we to say was gained by Abraham, our ancestor according to the flesh? For if Abraham was justified by works, he has something to boast about, but not before God. For what does the scripture say? "Abraham believed God, and it was reckoned to him as righteousness." Now to one who works, wages are not reckoned as a gift but as something due. But to one who without works trusts him who justifies the ungodly, such faith is reckoned as righteousness. (Romans 4:1-5, NRSV)

...Not Ashamed of the Gospel

Have you ever gotten credit for something you didn't do? At first, you might be tempted to not say anything—like when your sister washes the dishes and your mom comes home and thanks you. The more she goes on about how wonderful you are, the less you want to interrupt her to tell her the truth. So you say nothing. And you end up getting the credit for your sister's work.

Imagine for a moment what it would be like if your sister was right there and didn't say a word. She just stood there smiling and let you get the credit for what she did. You would have to conclude that either your sister's body had been taken over by aliens, or you had one awesome sister. In this passage, we learn a similar lesson about God.

The Jews felt that they had to work for God to reward them. But Paul says here that God has done the work for them. I'm sure that many of the Jews had the same reaction you would have had with your sister. They couldn't believe it. But they needed to believe it to receive God's blessing. Faith, not works, would give them their righteousness. And they needed that faith to receive God's reward.

...Not Ashamed of Digging Deeper

To justify his point, Paul uses Abraham, the father of the Jews, as his primary example. It was Abraham's belief in God, rather than his works for God, that made him righteous.

Abraham's greatest task was to believe. That is the same task that faces us all.

The more faith Abraham had, the more God did in Abraham's life. We'll learn more about that in the next passage. God wants to work the impossible in our lives but we have to believe the impossible to see it happen. It may feel like believing your sister would let you get the reward for her work. But with God, it's really true.

1. Have you ever gotten credit for something you didn't do? If so, how did it feel?

2. Is it hard for you to accept that you get the credit for something God has done for you? Why, or why not?

3. Why do we need to believe in order to receive favor from God? Can we earn it any other way? Why, or why not?

Against All Hope

Romans 4:13-25

Hoping against hope, he believed that he would become "the father of many nations," according to what was said, "So numerous shall your descendants be." He did not weaken in faith when he considered his own body, which was already as good as dead (for he was about a hundred years old), or when he considered the **...Not** *barrenness of Sarah's womb. No distrust made* **Ashamed** *him waver concerning the promise of God, but he* *grew strong in his faith as he gave glory to God,* **of the Gospel** *being fully convinced that God was able to do what he had promised. (Romans 4:18-21, NRSV)*

The story of Abraham is an amazing one. At the ripe young age of 75, he is visited by God and given a promise that he and his wife, Sarah, would bear a son. The only problem was that Sarah was 65 years old and infertile. God was calling Abraham to believe the impossible. And amazingly, Abraham did!

Ten years later, no son had been born. So Abraham and Sarah recruited a surrogate mother to help God out. But God let them know that the child they worked so hard to get was not the child God was going to give them. That child was still to come. Fifteen years later, Abraham, who was now 100, and Sarah, now 90, would conceive it. All Abraham could do was laugh. Wouldn't you?

One year later, their son was born. They named him Isaac, which means "laughter." God had required Abraham to have great faith so that Abraham could see God do great things. And the miracle of Isaac's birth clearly points to the power of God.

That's the God Paul writes about in this passage. **...Not Ashamed of Digging Deeper** And this same God is at work today.

For years, I dreamed of finding a husband; and I trusted that God would provide him. By the time I got to my 30s, I was a little concerned. I still believed that God would bring him, but how much longer would it be? When I turned 40, I felt that it would take a miracle for me to still be a bride. But that's exactly what God was waiting for.

In my forty-first year, I was approached by a stranger who told me that the Lord had not forgotten me and was going to bring me a husband. Three months later, I met a wonderful man named Brian; and four months later, he asked me to be his wife.

I could have been a 25-year-old bride with a normal story. Instead, I'm a 42-year-old bride-to-be with a miracle. And I relate to Abraham and Sarah. At 100 and 90, they became parents for the very first time. Their story is a testimony of faith. So is mine.

1. Why do you think God waited so long to give Abraham and Sarah a son?

...Not Ashamed of Living for Christ

2. Why do you think God is so interested in building our faith?

3. On a scale of 1–10 (with 1 being no faith and 10 being lots of faith), how much faith do you have?

How much faith would you like to have?

The Gift Nobody Wants

Romans 5:1-5

> *Therefore, since we have been justified through faith, we have peace with God through our Lord Jesus Christ, through whom we have gained access by faith into this grace in which we now stand. And we rejoice in the hope of the glory of God. Not only so, but we also rejoice in our sufferings, because we know that suffering produces perseverance; perseverance, character; and character, hope. And hope does not disappoint us, because God has poured out his love into our hearts by the Holy Spirit, whom he has given us.*
> *(Romans 5:1-5, NIV)*

...Not Ashamed of the Gospel

Have you ever wondered why God allows us to suffer? It seems so unfair and so unlike God that we feel abandoned when we go through it—until we look at the truths of this passage.

Paul doesn't see suffering as a curse. In fact, the way he describes it, it's more like a gift. He says that when sufferings happen, we should rejoice! Rejoice? How is that possible? Tolerate, maybe. (At least it's better than whining.) But rejoice?

It seems pretty unrealistic, until we are told what suffering can produce. Paul says that suffering produces perseverance—and it's true. When you're suffering, you learn to endure—usually because you have no choice. The only way to learn how to go through a hard time is to actually go through it. There is no way to practice.

Perseverance produces character. My fiancé, Brian, knows that firsthand. When he became a Marine officer, he didn't dress up and imagine what it would be like to be a soldier. He spent hours in the desert, being one. He was given very

...Not Ashamed of Digging Deeper

little water or food. He slept in a ditch. He went 26 days without a shower. (I'm glad I didn't know him then.) The way he learned discipline and strength was through pain and perseverance. And his character was developed along the way.

God wants us to develop that same character. So we shouldn't think that our suffering is for nothing, because of what that pain will produce.

Without suffering, we would be selfish, undisciplined people, unprepared to face hard times and unable to really minister to others in their times of suffering. When we suffer, we develop what we need to be God's agents in the world. And this gives us hope for ourselves and others, because God uses this process to fill our hearts with love.

So when you suffer, it's OK to be sad. But you can rejoice in the knowledge that God *will use it* to help you and others grow.

1. How can God use suffering for good in your life?

...Not Ashamed of Living for Christ

Based on this Scripture passage, what happens to us when we suffer?

2. Have you ever experienced great suffering? If so, what effect did it have in your life?

3. What is the hope that comes from suffering?

Have you ever experienced this? If so, how? If not, why not?

His Life for Ours

Romans 5:6-11

For while we were still weak, at the right time Christ died for the ungodly. Indeed, rarely will anyone die for a righteous person—though perhaps for a good person someone might actually dare to die. But God proves his love for us in that while we still were sinners Christ died for us....For if while we were

...Not
Ashamed
of the Gospel

were reconciled to God through the death of his Son, much more surely, having been reconciled, will we be saved by his life.
(Romans 5:6-8, 10, NRSV)

In World War II, millions of Jews were sent to concentration camps, where they were tortured and killed in unspeakable ways. In one such camp, a human drama took place that was witnessed by only a few individuals. But it captured the attention of many after the war.

A Catholic priest named Father Kolbe had been taken to a camp, and one day was ordered to strip naked and line up with the Jews for a random inspection. The Germans were going to select ten prisoners to be moved to a special cell, where they would be given no food or water until they died.

Father Kolbe breathed a sigh of relief as the Germans passed him over. The man next to him was not so lucky. As this man was taken, Father Kolbe heard him say, "My poor wife! My poor children!" He knew what

he must do. Father Kolbe stepped out of line and approached the commandant. "Sir," he said, "I would like to die in place of that man." The German official stared at the priest. When he saw the priest's aging body, the official decided to allow the switch. The man was shoved back in line, and Father Kolbe took his place.

...Not
Ashamed
of Digging
Deeper

Verse 5:7 says that for a good person, someone might possibly dare to die. Father Kolbe did just that. I can only imagine how that man must have felt stepping back in line while a stranger took his place. But imagine for a moment if the story had taken a different turn. What if a German official was

36

suddenly betrayed and taken with the Jewish prisoners. What if another man stepped out and said "I would like to die in place of that German official." Imagine the prisoners' faces as this man stepped out to take the place of an enemy. Imagine the face of the German official!

In a very real sense, that's what it was like when Jesus Christ died on the cross. He didn't wait until we deserved his sacrifice. He did it when we didn't deserve it. "While we still were sinners Christ died for us" (verse 8). That's the man who took our place.

1. Has someone ever made a significant sacrifice for you? If so, how did it feel? (If you can't think of anyone, think about your parents).

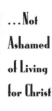

...Not Ashamed of Living for Christ

2. How is Jesus' sacrifice for us different than the sacrifices we make for others?

3. How does knowing that Jesus died for you while you were a sinner affect your faith? Is it hard for you to believe? Why?

The First and Second Man

Romans 5:12-21

...Not Ashamed of the Gospel

Therefore, just as sin entered the world through one man, and death through sin, and in this way death came to all men, because all sinned—for before the law was given, sin was in the world. But sin is not taken into account when there is no law....

The law was added so that the trespass might increase. But where sin increased, grace increased all the more, so that, just as sin reigned in death, so also grace might reign through righteousness to bring eternal life through Jesus Christ our Lord. (Romans 5:12-13, 20-21, NIV)

It's hard to imagine the mind of God when Adam was created. But I'd bet that God would have liked for Adam to have made one different choice. When God said that Adam could eat from any tree, except one, it didn't take Adam very long to decide that it was the one tree he wanted most. So he disobeyed God. And from that decision on, the descendants of Adam have been following his example.

Perhaps God had in mind that people would choose obedience. But the fact is, God gave us a choice. In giving us freedom, God allowed for the possibility that we would choose *not* to obey, and that's exactly what we have done. It may have begun with Adam, but it continues today with us.

Though God's original intention was to give life, the result of disobedience led to death. But God is so loving that another plan was already in the works. Paul says that this plan involved a second man, and that man was Jesus Christ.

Like Adam, Jesus was given a crucial choice. But his choice was much more difficult.

...Not Ashamed of Digging Deeper

Adam was asked to simply not eat from one of the trees of the garden. Jesus had to suffer and die on a cross. When Jesus was praying on the night before his death, he said "Father, if you are willing, remove this cup from me." In other words, "Please, Daddy, stop this from happening!" After Jesus was met with silence, he said "Not my will but yours be done" (Luke 22:42). In that brief statement of obedience, Jesus undid the disobedience of Adam. And by going to the cross, he undid the disobedience of us all.

Adam paved the way for disobedience and death. Jesus paved the way for obedience and life. By trusting Jesus to lead our lives, we are given the road beyond death to everlasting life. Through Adam, the first man, we received death; but through Jesus, the second man, we inherit the road to heaven.

1. Do you think that Adam is responsible for all our sin? Why?

...Not Ashamed of Living for Christ

In what way is Adam like all of us?

2. Have you ever done something you knew God didn't want you to do? What resulted from the sin?

3. How does this passage show us the importance of trusting Christ to lead us?

Do you feel that you've done that?

In what areas do you need help?

New Body Parts

Romans 6:1-14

In the same way, count yourselves dead to sin but alive to God in Christ Jesus. Therefore do not let sin reign in your mortal body so that you obey its evil desires. Do not offer the parts of your body to sin, as instruments of wickedness, but rather offer yourselves to God, as those who have been brought from death to life; and offer the parts of your body to him as instruments of righteousness. For sin shall not be your master, because you are not under law, but under grace. (Romans 6:11-14, NIV)

...Not Ashamed of the Gospel

A few weeks ago, I was in a car accident. Thankfully, no one was hurt, except my car. It resembled an accordion when it was towed away. It took three weeks for the shop to repair the damage; but when I finally got it back, it ran better than before. It was almost like getting a new car.

Imagine if I had gone to the mechanic and said, "I know that my car needs to be fixed, but please don't replace any of the body parts. I'm used to the old ones, so I want to keep them the way they are." The mechanic would have probably thought to himself, "I never believed those blonde jokes till now!"

It seems like a ridiculous illustration, but it's a little like what Paul is talking about in this passage. When we give our lives to Christ, we trade in our old selves (which belong to sin) and become new creations (who belong to Christ). So our body parts have to become new too.

This can be painful, because we're used to the way the old body parts run. Our legs have taken us places we no longer want to go.

...Not Ashamed of Digging Deeper

Our eyes have looked at things we no longer want to see. Our brains have been filled with thoughts we no longer want to think. We know that God needs to change us, but it's tempting to keep our body parts working the way they did before. It's much more comfortable and convenient.

This doesn't work for long though. Once you invite Christ into your life, he'll keep working on those body parts to fit your new self. You may try to ignore his voice, but he'll keep speaking to your heart until you're ready to hear what needs to change. Soon you'll find that your new self runs much better than your old self—kind of like my car.

Until then, it will be like trying to drive a new car with all the old body parts. And that's not a smart way to travel. Or live.

1. What does it mean to offer the parts of your body to sin?

...Not Ashamed of Living for Christ

What does it mean to offer the parts of your body to righteousness?

2. Which parts of your body are offered for righteousness?

Which are not?

3. What body parts need to be repaired (or replaced)?

How can you begin the process of letting Jesus repair you?

A New Owner

Romans 6:15-22

What then? Should we sin because we are not under law but under grace? By no means! Do you not know that if you present yourselves to anyone as obedient slaves, you are slaves of the one whom you obey, either of sin, which leads to death, or of obedience, which leads to righteousness? But thanks be to God that you,

...Not Ashamed of the Gospel

having once been slaves of sin, have become obedient from the heart to the form of teaching to which you were entrusted and that you, having been set free from sin, have become slaves of righteousness. (Romans 6:15-18, NRSV)

Years ago, Bob Dylan wrote a hit song called "You Gotta Serve Somebody." The premise of the song was that all of us are serving someone, even if we're unaware of it. That's what Paul talks about in this passage.

You show who you're serving by the way you spend your time. You show who you're serving by the way you spend your money. You show who you're serving by the sacrifices you make. And you show who you're serving by the things you're compelled to do. These things define your master.

A lot of people say that they don't want to become Christians because they don't want to lose their freedom. But they never really had it to begin with. We are all slaves to something. And even if we never consciously chose a

master, our actions and habits show us who or what we serve. It's just a matter of identifying what it is.

When you become a Christian, you don't lose your freedom— you gain it. Jesus Christ is the only one who can be

...Not Ashamed of Digging Deeper

your master without taking your freedom away. Ironically, people who think that they're free by "doing their own thing" are actually trapped by the very thing they're doing. Most addicts think that they could stop at anytime; but in reality, they are bound to their habit. But Jesus' way of controlling you is by setting you free.

When Jesus becomes your master, he sets you free *from*

sin. But you are also set free *for* righteousness. It's kind of like starting a new diet. At first, you crave the stuff you used to eat; but after a while, you develop new cravings and you actually start liking food that's good for you. Soon you don't even miss the old food. Because you're eating the food your body needs to work best.

Jesus Christ knows how you work best. When you make him your master, he'll help you become the person you were meant to be. You gotta serve somebody. Make it him!

1. What do your time and money say about who and what you serve?

Do they show that you serve God? How?

2. Would you describe yourself as free? Why?

3. Is Jesus your master? If so, how is this reflected in your life? If not, what is?

The Death That Gave Us Life

Romans 6:23

For the wages of sin is death, but the free gift of God is eternal life in Christ Jesus our Lord. (Romans 6:23, NRSV)

...Not
Ashamed
of the Gospel

Years ago, I heard a story that I never forgot. It was about a drawbridge operator whose job it was to raise and lower a bridge so that boats could pass through the channel. However, this bridge served a dual purpose. There were train tracks running across it, so the operator had to be sure to time this process to meet the schedule of the train.

One day, the drawbridge operator took his 8-year-old son with him to work. Much to the boy's delight, a boat was making it's way down the river and he was able to watch his dad push the button to raise the bridge. While his dad was busy timing the bridge with the approaching vessel, the boy slipped out of his father's lap and crawled under the bridge to get a better look. Just then, the drawbridge operator heard a train whistle. He looked at his watch. The train was off schedule, but there it was barreling down the tracks toward the bridge.

The drawbridge operator reasoned that he had just enough time to lower the bridge for the train to make it across. As he started to push the button,

...Not
Ashamed
of Digging
Deeper

he saw his little boy crawling on a beam under the bridge. He cried out to him, but the approaching train drowned out his voice. In one split second, the man realized that he would not have time to get his son and lower the bridge. He was forced to make a choice.

With tears streaming down his face, the man pushed the button to lower the bridge. As the train sped by, the passengers smiled

44

and waved, unaware of the drama that had just occurred. The man they were waving at had just spared their death, and he sacrificed his own son to do it.

This story is not unlike what God did for us. The magnitude of God's free gift is stated boldly by Paul in Romans 6:23.

It may seem strange to have a whole devotion about only one verse. But this verse deserves it. Now you know why.

1. What would you have done if you were the man in this story?

...Not Ashamed of Living for Christ

2. What parallels can you draw from this story and what God did for us?

What similarities do you see?

What differences?

3. What can you do this week to show your appreciation to God for sacrificing Jesus for your life?

Service From the Heart

Romans 7:1-6

So, my brothers [and sisters], you also died to the law through the body of Christ, that you might belong to another, to him who was raised from the dead, in order that we might bear fruit to God. For when we were controlled by the sinful nature, the sinful passions aroused by the law were at work in our bodies, so that we bore fruit for death. But now, by dying to what once bound us, we have been released from the law so that we serve in the new way of the Spirit, and not in the old way of the written code.
(Romans 7:4-6, NIV)

...Not Ashamed of the Gospel

Have you ever noticed how much easier it is to do something when you want to, rather than when you have to? One of the chores I hated was cleaning my room, but my mom always made me do it. The only time I didn't mind doing it was when she didn't ask me. Somehow, when I could clean my room when I wanted to, instead of when she made me, I didn't mind doing it at all.

That's a little like what Paul is talking about in this passage. The Law is laid out in the Old Testament—the same way your mom or dad lays out your chores. It was a big list of things God wanted us to do. But now, Paul says, God has released us from the Law. We no longer have to obey the Law to win God's favor. We just have to commit ourselves to Jesus Christ. The irony is that not having to obey makes us want to all the more.

One reason is that we realize how much Jesus loves us, and we want to return that love. Love is a great motivator to serve. Have you noticed that when you fall in love, how suddenly you're at that person's beck and call, ready to do just about anything? If your new love has a problem, you are always there to talk, no matter how much time it requires. Your schedule miraculously clears whenever he or she is around. Your sole desire is to please your new love—not because you have to, but because you want to.

...Not Ashamed of Digging Deeper

That's how it is when we fall in love with Jesus. We don't please him because we have to; we please him because we want to—and we are compelled because of his love. The fact that he died for us, with no strings attached, makes us want to serve him the same way. The Spirit motivates us do it.

When we do serve Christ from our hearts, it doesn't even feel like service at all. We are the ones who are blessed. That's God's secret surprise.

1. Have you ever been blessed by serving someone else? If so, when? What did it feel like?

2. What's the difference between serving because of the Law and serving because of the Spirit?

Which do you do more?

3. What is one act of service you could do this week to show your love for God?

The Direction We Need

Romans 7:7-13

...Not
Ashamed
of the Gospel

What shall we say, then? Is the law sin? Certainly not! Indeed I would not have known what sin was except through the law. For I would not have known what coveting really was if the law had not said, "Do not covet." But sin, seizing the opportunity afforded by the commandment, produced in me every kind of covetous desire. For apart from law, sin is dead. Once I was alive apart from law; but when the commandment came, sin sprang to life and I died. I found that the very commandment that was intended to bring life actually brought death. (Romans 7:7-10, NIV)

Have you ever been studying for a test and realized that the more you studied, the less you knew? You end up feeling worse than before you started. At least, before you started, you didn't know what you didn't know. Now you realize how much you have to do, and it makes you want to give up.

That's the experience Paul is talking about in this passage. He says that knowing God's Law doesn't make you feel better; it makes you feel worse, because it identifies a sinful part of you that you didn't even know existed. By reading God's commandments, you realize how many things are wrong that you didn't even know were wrong in the first place. And knowing that those things are wrong makes the struggle even worse.

Let me explain that last statement. When you can stay up as late as you want, you might choose to go to bed early. But when you are told that you have to go to bed, suddenly you have this huge temptation to stay up late. Or take food, for instance. When you can eat whatever you want, you eat when  you're hungry and stop when you're full. But the minute you go on a diet, food is all you can think about. What wasn't a temptation before has now become a temptation—all because you're trying to restrain.

...Not
Ashamed
of Digging
Deeper

That, Paul says, is the effect that the Law has on our lives. Not only does it expose our sins, it creates more of a desire to sin now that we know what's wrong. So what is the solution—to get rid of the Law? Paul says, "By no means." In other words, "No way!" We need the Law to guide us, even if we can't do what it's telling us to do. It's like a compass for our lives, because it shows us how far we are from the path we need to take. Without it, we would be lost.

But we need more than a compass to get us where we need to go. That's what Paul is leading up to in this passage. The Law can direct our path, but it can't keep us on the path. For that, we need a Guide.

1. What's the difference between a compass and a guide?

...Not Ashamed of Living for Christ

Which one is more like the Law? Why?

2. If you had to describe God's Law as a compass, would you say that you use your compass all the time, some of the time, or not at all? Why?

3. Does the Law inspire you or frustrate you? Why?

How does it help or hinder your relationship with God?

The Lifelong Struggle

Romans 7:14-25

I know that nothing good lives in me, that is, in my sinful nature. For I have the desire to do what is good, but I cannot carry it out. For what I do is not the good I want to do; no, the evil I do not want to do—this I keep on doing. Now if I do what I do not want to do, it is no longer I who do it, but it is sin living in me that does it....

What a wretched man I am! Who will rescue me from this body of death?
(Romans 7:18-20, 24, NIV)

...Not Ashamed of the Gospel

This might be my favorite passage, because it helps me know that I'm not alone. The struggle Paul talks about in this passage is the same struggle I feel—no matter how long I've been a Christian. Maybe you can relate too.

Paul has explained in previous chapters how Jesus has freed us from our sins. So you'd expect Paul to now describe his sinless life. Instead, Paul says, "I have the desire to do what is good, but I cannot carry it out" (verse 18). The tongue twisters of this passage describe Paul's struggle—that what he wants to do he cannot do—and he does the very things that he doesn't want to do. I would think that there was something wrong with him, except I find the same experience within myself. Do you?

People have the impression that Christians should be perfect. But the fact is that Christians live on the same plain as everyone else. We are not "spirit people" who float above the struggles of life. We are spirit-filled people who live in the midst of the struggles of life.

...Not Ashamed of Digging Deeper

One of the confusing things about being a Christian is realizing that you still battle with sin. You feel that you shouldn't struggle; or at least, that you shouldn't struggle as much. But sometimes you struggle even more. A battle rages inside you—and that's what is described in this passage. Two natures exist where there once was one, and they are competing for control of your actions. Your new nature is of the spirit; but instead of replacing your sin nature, it has come in to control your sin nature.

The good news is that this battle will not go on forever. Jesus assures that your new nature will win. In the meantime, you can call on him to guide you in the struggle. He knows what it's like. He fought it on the cross.

…Not Ashamed of Living for Christ

1. Have you ever felt the struggle Paul talks about in this passage? If so, when?

2. How do Paul's words make you feel about what it's like to be a Christian?

Do you agree with him? Why, or why not?

3. What does it mean to let Christ win the battle?

Is there a battle inside you that you need Christ to win?

The Battle of the Mind

Romans 8:1-11

For those who live according to the flesh set their minds on the things of the flesh, but those who live according to the Spirit set their minds on the things of the Spirit. To set the mind on the flesh is death, but to set the mind on the Spirit is life and peace. For this reason the mind that is set on the flesh is hostile to God; it does not submit to God's law—indeed it cannot, and those who are in the flesh cannot please God.
(Romans 8:5-8, NRSV)

...Not Ashamed of the Gospel

I can't stand fights. It amazes me that people pay money to sit around a ring and watch two grown men—and now women—beat each other up. But I have to admit that I did kind of get into boxing when the movie *Rocky* came out. Something about that movie drew me in, and I ended up cheering at every one of his fights.

The excitement of *Rocky* might be a little before your time, but you may have heard the song "Eye of the Tiger" or seen the movies on video or DVD. The message of every Rocky movie was always the same: Rocky's strength came from his focus. It didn't matter how much of an underdog he was or how treacherous his opponent. The battle was won or lost by Rocky's state of mind when he entered the fight. This is a great illustration for what Paul describes in this passage.

In Romans 7, we learned that there are two natures struggling within us. But Romans 8 tells us that our minds have much to do with which nature wins. Paul says that where you set your mind will make all the difference in how you live.

...Not Ashamed of Digging Deeper

It's nearly impossible to have your mind set on God and enjoy sinning. Thoughts of God make sin a lot less fun. That's why it's a great strategy if you're trying to stop sinning.

The hard part about battling our sins is that we can beat our opponents only one at a time. Once we conquer one sin, another takes it's place. In that respect, it's a lot like boxing. Rocky never had more than one opponent in the ring; but as soon as he beat that opponent, he had to face the challenge of someone else. However, the most important lesson he learned was between battles. He had to keep "the eye of the tiger," because his focus determined his victory.

It's the same for us. But it's not the "eye of the tiger" we need—it's the mind of Christ. If our focus stays on him, the victory is ours.

1. How much does your mind affect what you do?

...Not Ashamed of Living for Christ

Would you say that it affects you positively or negatively? Why?

2. Have you ever done something you didn't think you could do because you put your mind to it?

What did it feel like?

3. Is there a sin you're struggling with right now in your life?

How can having the mind of Christ help you conquer that sin?

Children of God

Romans 8:12-17

For you did not receive a spirit of slavery to fall back into fear, but you have received a spirit of adoption. When we cry, "Abba! Father!" it is that very spirit bearing witness with our spirit that we are children of God, and if children, then heirs, heirs of God and joint heirs with Christ—if, in fact, we suffer with him so that we may also be glorified with him.
(Romans 8:15-17, NRSV)

...Not Ashamed of the Gospel

Have you ever seen a new mother and father with their child? Everything the child does is a monumental event. First smile, first burp, first step ... and out come the cameras, the videotape, the postings on the website.

I was with a friend when her youngest child was being potty trained, and the whole family was home to participate in this grand occasion. There was Will, sitting on the potty seat, his parents standing right at the door. They started chanting "Come on, Will! Come on, Will!" I looked over and saw Will, with a bright red face, pushing with all of his might. Finally, the moment came, and Will delivered. His mom and dad started dancing, and singing, and high-fiving. I looked over at Will and I could tell that he was thinking, "If this is all I gotta do to get this kind of reaction, life is going to be a piece of cake."

Will was loved, and his mom and dad wanted to celebrate every step of growth because he was their child. Paul says that's what God is like with us. Not that God gets that excited  ...Not Ashamed of Digging Deeper every time we go to the bathroom, but God rejoices over every victory we achieve.

We are God's children. We even get to call God "Abba"—the Aramaic word for "Daddy." In other words, Paul says that we can cry out to our Daddy for whatever we need and that God is always there to guide us and strengthen us as we grow.

This is what helps us in our daily struggles. We have a God

who celebrates us, loves us, and helps us in our time of need. We will go through struggles and pain. We may wonder sometimes whether we'll make it. But one day, we'll receive our inheritance as God's children; and the victory will be ours.

Then there will be some party in heaven! And it will even be bigger than Will's.

1. How does thinking of God as a parent deepen your understanding of God's love?

What kind of relationship do you have with your parents?

2. Do you think that God spends more time celebrating the things you do right or criticizing the things you do wrong? Why?

3. What step of growth may God want you to take?

What do you need to do in order to take that step?

All Things Work Together

Romans 8:18-30

I consider that the sufferings of this present time are not worth comparing with the glory about to be revealed to us.... But if we hope for what we do not see, we wait for it with patience.

Likewise the Spirit helps us in our weakness; for we do not know how to pray as we ought, but that very Spirit intercedes with **...Not** *sighs too deep for words. And God, who searches the heart, knows what is the mind of the Spirit,* **Ashamed** *because the Spirit intercedes for the saints* **of the Gospel** *according to the will of God.*

We know that all things work together for good for those who love God, who are called according to his purpose. (Romans 8:18, 25-28, NRSV)

Have you ever made chocolate chip cookies? It's kind of a shock when you realize what goes into them. You start with flour, sugar, baking soda, and salt. Then you add butter, vanilla, and eggs. Finally, you add the chocolate; and you combine all those things to make your cookies.

Before you head to the kitchen to make them, look over that list of ingredients again. Taken separately, only two ingredients taste good. The rest you wouldn't want to put in your mouth. But you need all of these ingredients to make your cookies. And this provides a great analogy for what Paul describes in this passage.

We've been hearing about the struggles we face in our lives and how one day the struggle will end. But here Paul gives us a picture of what God is *doing* with our struggles. Taken separately,

our sufferings feel unwanted and unnecessary—much like some of the ingredients of a chocolate chip cookie. We wonder why God allows them. But we need those things to become all God is making us to be. Because it is our present sufferings that will bring forth the glory that will one day be revealed.

...Not Ashamed of Digging Deeper

All things work together for good. That's what Paul says in verse 28. The "all things" that work together are individually not that great. Sometimes they're awful. They can even make us groan. But when they're put together, all our sufferings will eventually form our best self. And that's our hope—that God is going to use our pain to achieve our glory.

So the next time you eat a chocolate chip cookie right out of the oven, think about what it took to make it. Maybe it will help you remember what God is doing with you.

1. If you had to compare your life to a chocolate chip cookie, what would the good ingredients be?

What would the bad ingredients be?

2. Have you ever seen anything good come out of suffering? When?

3. How can this passage help you have a new perspective on the bad things in your life?

Write down a specific struggle you are going through and make a list of any good things that could come from your struggle.

More Than Conquerors

Romans 8:31-39

What, then, shall we say in response to this? If God is for us, who can be against us? ...

No, in all these things we are more than conquerors through him who loved us. For I am convinced that neither death nor life, neither angels nor demons, neither the present nor the future, nor any powers, neither height nor depth, nor anything else in all creation, will be able to separate us from the love of God that is in Christ Jesus our Lord. (Romans 8:31, 37-39, NIV)

...Not Ashamed of the Gospel

B*raveheart* was a great movie. If you didn't see it, you should rent it. It is the true story about Scotland's quest for independence from England and how William Wallace, "Braveheart," led his people to fight for a cause that was bigger than themselves. Some of the most stirring scenes showed Wallace standing before the Scottish army, inspiring them to face their enemy with courage and might. But he never sent them to battle alone. He always went with them.

We have a God who does the same thing. In the battles of our lives, Jesus does not leave us alone. He is with us. Whether we face trouble or hardship or persecution or death—nothing can separate us from Christ. No matter how lonely we may feel, we are not abandoned. Jesus is with us in every difficulty we face.

This passage indicates that sometimes the battles we face are bigger than ourselves. We face physical and spiritual wars in this world. Paul wants us to know that in every battle, Jesus is on our side. He intercedes on our behalf. He does not cheer us from the sidelines. He is right there with us in the battle.

...Not Ashamed of Digging Deeper

It may seem strange to think that Jesus could be present in the dark battles of life—until we think about the cross. In that dark moment when God allowed Jesus to die, Jesus faced pain and separation and death. But he conquered them all. Three days later he rose from the dead. And he won the victory—not only for himself, but for those of us who follow him.

Only by dying could Jesus show us that even in death, we can be more than conquerors. So how can we be afraid?

1. Have you ever felt God fighting with you in your struggles?

...Not Ashamed of Living for Christ

Did it feel like God was for you or against you? Why?

2. How do we know that God is with us if we can't see God?

In what ways do we know that God is there?

3. What battle do you face right now that you need God's help with?

How can this passage help you know that God is with you in the battle?

Children of Promise

Romans 9:1-13

It is not as though the word of God had failed. For not all Israelites truly belong to Israel, and not all of Abraham's children are his true descendants; but "It is through Isaac that descendants shall be named for you." This means that it is not the children of the flesh who are the children of God, but the children of the promise are counted as descendants.
(Romans 9:6-8, NRSV)

...Not
Ashamed
of the Gospel

In the next three chapters of Romans, Paul really shows us his heart for the Jews. It is his greatest desire, even at the expense of his own salvation, that the Jews would be saved.

Paul is so concerned that the Jews come to accept the gospel of Jesus Christ that he has "great sorrow and unceasing anguish" (verse 2) for them to see the truth. What an example for us to follow in reaching out to our friends! We should long for the people we love to know the truth. And like Paul, we should do whatever we can do to help them see it.

The first thing Paul does is find a connecting point that the Jews can relate to from their history. So Abraham is brought back into the picture to make his case. Paul has already used Abraham to make it clear that faith, rather than the Law, brings righteousness. This time

Paul uses him to explain that God's children are not chosen because they are Jewish; they are chosen because of their faith.

It was Abraham's child Isaac, born out of faith, who inherited God's promise. Abraham had other children who were born in a natural way. But Isaac was born God's way, and he was the one who inherited God's blessing. Through that miraculous event, God made it clear that children who inherit the promise are born out of faith, and Paul wants the Jews to see that.

...Not
Ashamed
of Digging
Deeper

The Jews have to come to grips with the fact that their heritage is not the source of their blessing. They too must be children of faith. Like the Gentiles, they must trust Jesus Christ for their salvation. God has no grandchildren—only children.

That is an important lesson for us to remember too. You can't be a Christian through your parents' faith. You can't be a Christian because of where you come from. You can only be a Christian because of *your faith* in Jesus Christ alone.

1. Why is it important to us that Isaac was the chosen child of Abraham and not another child who was born in the natural way?

2. Do you see any parallel between the birth of Isaac and the way we become Christians?

3. Why doesn't God have grandchildren?

What does that tell you about the importance of individual faith?

Would you describe your faith that way? Why?

The Unfairness of Grace

Romans 9:14-29

...Not Ashamed of the Gospel

What then are we to say? Is there injustice on God's part? By no means! For he says to Moses, "I will have mercy on whom I have mercy, and I will have compassion on whom I have compassion." So it depends not on human will or exertion, but on God who shows mercy. For the scripture says to Pharaoh, "I have raised you up for the very purpose of showing my power in you, so that my name may be proclaimed in all the earth." So then he has mercy on whomever he chooses, and he hardens the heart of whomever he chooses. (Romans 9:14-18, NRSV)

God's grace seems unfair—at least, according to this passage. But let me ask you something. Do you really want fairness from God?

If we received fairness from God, we would all be dead. That's what our sins deserve. Instead, God has given us what we don't deserve—an opportunity for life. It's unfair that Jesus Christ had to die an innocent death. It's unfair that he had to take our guilt on his shoulders. It's unfair that he bled on our behalf. We don't have to pay for our own sins, because God has done it for us. *That's* what's unfair!

When we first read this passage, we are tempted to question God's fairness. But what would it be like if God were really fair? We might think it's unfair that God allows people to choose death. But what's really unfair is that God

allows people to choose life. Fairness is when people get what they deserve. Thankfully, we serve an unfair God—and we get what we *don't* deserve!

Paul's words make it clear that some will choose not to follow Christ. So this

...Not Ashamed of Digging Deeper

passage raises the questions for us: Why would God allow that? If God knows what we'll choose before we choose it, isn't it God's fault if we don't choose correctly?

One of the mysteries of God's design is that God is sovereign, yet we are free. It doesn't seem like we could be free if God knows what we're going to do. But *we* don't know what we're going to do, so we still have the freedom to choose. The fact that we *can* choose to follow Christ is a sign of God's mercy. The fact that some don't and suffer the consequences is a sign of God's fairness.

So the question is, Do you really want God to be more fair? Not me. I'll settle for the unfairness of grace.

...Not Ashamed of Living for Christ

1. Would you describe grace as unfair or fair? Why?

2. Have you ever wondered why some people accept God's mercy and others reject it?

3. What would happen to the world if God were more fair?

What would happen to you?

You Gotta Have Faith

Romans 9:30-33

What then are we to say? Gentiles, who did not strive for righteousness, have attained it, that is, righteousness through faith; but Israel, who did strive for the righteousness that is based on the law, did not succeed in fulfilling that law. Why not? Because they did not strive for it on the basis of faith, but as if it were based on works. They have stumbled over the stumbling stone, as it is written,

"See, I am laying in Zion a stone
that will make people stumble,
a rock that will make them fall,
and whoever believes in him
will not be put to shame."
(Romans 9:30-33, NRSV)

...Not Ashamed of the Gospel

In the early 1980s, a popular songwriter came out with a hit tune. The beat was very catchy, and he repeated the same words over and over throughout the song. "You gotta have faith, faith, faith.... You gotta have faith, faith, faith!" Although I'm pretty sure Paul wouldn't have liked the other lyrics this guy wrote, this is one phrase that he would have loved. It's a great theme song for this passage.

Paul says that there is one thing Jews and Gentiles have in common: They've got to have faith. This was easier for the Gentiles to accept, because they didn't have any other way to get to God. But the Jews were used to approaching God through the Law. They couldn't accept that all God wanted them to do was have faith in Christ. So Christ was a stumbling block to the Jews.

Paul refers to Old Testament Scripture to let the Jews know that God had the redemptive work of Jesus planned from the beginning. The verses from Isaiah show God's intention in bringing Christ, and they also indicate that the Jews

...Not Ashamed of Diggin Deeper

would have a problem with it. Christ is referred to as "a stone that will make people stumble" (verse 33). By the amount of time Paul spends convincing the Jews to accept Christ, we can see that Isaiah was right.

It's strange that the Jews would be so blind to prophecy coming straight from their Scriptures. But they were used to seeing God a certain way.

Paul himself was a Jew, so he understands their stubbornness. But he will not give up.

That's why he keeps pounding out the message over and over again. It's like a song that goes through his head. And he'll repeat it until his message is heard.

"You gotta have faith."

...Not Ashamed of Living for Christ

1. Why is our faith so important to God?

Do you think that faith is more important than our actions? Why?

2. What do you think it means to be righteous by faith?

Do you think that it's a greater righteousness than being righteous by works?

3. Would you describe yourself as righteous by faith? Why?

Misdirected Zeal

Romans 10:1-8

Brothers and sisters, my heart's desire and prayer to God for them is that they may be saved. I can testify that they have a zeal for God, but it is not enlightened. For, being ignorant of the righteousness that comes from God, and seeking to establish their own, they have not submitted to God's righteousness. For Christ is the end of the law so that there may be righteousness for everyone who believes. (Romans 10:1-4, NRSV)

...Not Ashamed of the Gospel

A terrorist referred to as "The Shoe Bomber" was recently tried in court. His crime? He tried to blow up a plane, but failed because he was stopped by some brave crew members and passengers. Nobody was hurt, but he was convicted and sentenced to life in prison.

The sentence might seem rather severe, except for the unrepentant zeal the terrorist showed in court. Several times he indicated that if he was given the same chance, he'd try it again. It was clear that he saw himself as a hero of his beliefs. But the courtroom saw him as he was: a criminal.

This story illustrates the extreme of what can happen when zeal is misdirected. Paul experienced that himself. In his days as a devout Jew, Paul stood by and watched approvingly as Christians were tortured and

killed. He was almost as bad as a terrorist—and he felt that he was representing God.

But then Paul met the God he was seeking to represent. On the road to Damascus, Paul encountered Jesus Christ and realized that he had been wrong. From that moment on, Paul's zeal was redirected and put toward helping others see the truth. The same zeal he had as a Jew, he now had as a Christian. And he wanted other Jews to experience it too.

...Not Ashamed of Digging Deeper

The Jews were zealous for God, but their zeal was misdirected. It was leading them astray—not toward terrorism, like the shoe bomber, but toward wrong belief. Paul longed for them to redirect their zeal toward Jesus Christ.

Imagine what would happen today if some of the terrorists did that. They might be some of the most committed Christians in the world. It may be hard for us to picture. But then, look at Paul.

1. Have you ever seen someone with misdirected religious zeal? What actions showed zeal?

2. In what way do terrorists show an extreme form of misdirected zeal?

What do you think led them to be like that?

3. What kind of zeal for God do you have?

Do you need more zeal or less? Why?

The Way of Salvation

Romans 10:9-13

That if you confess with your mouth, "Jesus is Lord," and believe in your heart that God raised him from the dead, you will be saved. For it is with your heart that you believe and are justified, and it is with your mouth that you confess and are saved. As the Scripture says, "Anyone who trusts in him will never be put to shame."
(Romans 10:9-11, NIV)

...Not

Ashamed

of the Gospel

Have you ever wondered how to become a Christian? Everything you need to know is in this passage. It's not about going to church or being a good person. These things help you *live* your faith, but they don't give you your faith. Your faith comes from belief in Jesus Christ, and you have to make that confession for yourself.

Your confession can happen in a variety of ways. You can stand up at a conference or simply pray with a friend. You can proclaim it at your confirmation or proclaim it at your baptism. You can walk forward during an altar call or raise your hand from your seat. No one method exists for becoming a Christian, but there is only one way.

You must confess with your mouth that Jesus is Lord and believe in your heart that God raised him from the dead. It is not enough to do one or the other. Your confession is what strengthens your belief. Think about it: When you make a commitment, you're more likely to remember it if you tell someone about it. Otherwise, you'll probably forget. That's why it's so important to make a confession of faith.

...Not

Ashamed

of Digging

Deeper

The good news is that it's never too late. I was a senior in high school when I made my confession of faith; and even though I had believed in God my whole life, something happened after I made my confession. Standing up in front of my friends strengthened my belief, and it was then that I really committed my life to Christ.

So if you can't remember a time when you made a confession of faith, why not do it right now? When you confess Jesus' name before others, you can be assured of one thing—he'll do the same for you before God.

1. According to verse 9, there are two things you are supposed to do to become a Christian. What are they?

...Not Ashamed of Living for Christ

2. Have you done both of these things? If so, when?

Did they happen at the same time or at different times?

3. Do you think that it's important to God that we make a confession of faith? Why?

If you haven't made a confession of faith, do you want to? When could you do it? How will you do it?

Called to Proclaim

Romans 10:14-21

How, then, can they call on the one they have not believed in? And how can they believe in the one of whom they have not heard? And how can they hear without someone preaching to them? And how can they preach unless they are sent? As it is written, "How beautiful are the feet of those who bring good news!"

...Not Ashamed of the Gospel

But not all the Israelites accepted the good news. For Isaiah says, "Lord, who has believed our message?" Consequently, faith comes from hearing the message, and the message is heard through the word of Christ. (Romans 10:14-17, NIV)

Some things we should keep to ourselves. Our faith is not one of them. In this passage, Paul says that part of the reason we are to confess with our mouths that "Jesus is Lord" is for the salvation of others. Because our witness might be the reason someone else comes to believe.

There are many ways to share your faith, but one way is simply to tell others your story. Sometimes hearing about your faith makes people want to experience it for themselves. The best way to start is to tell people why your faith is important to you. If they ask questions, you can tell them more. If they don't ask questions, they might think about it—and you've planted a seed God can water at a later time.

Another way to share your faith is to tell people God's story—the gospel—the news that God sent Jesus Christ to die for our sins so that we can have everlasting life. You may feel uncomfortable sharing God's story, because you don't know how to do it very well. But God will use what you do know if you are willing to step out in faith.

...Not Ashamed of Digging Deeper

When you do step out and share, you are not responsible for people's responses. That part is up to God. But no matter what happens, every effort you make is beautiful to God (verse 15). So, whether you have all the right words or not, God can use you if you are willing.

The last thing to remember is that your life might be the first gospel someone hears. So the way you live may be your most powerful witness of all. Saint Augustine said it best, "Preach the gospel at all times. If necessary, use words." Then watch what God can do.

1. Do you think that all Christians are supposed to share their faith? Why?

...Not Ashamed of Living for Christ

2. Have you ever shared your faith? If so, what happened? If not, why not?

3. Is there anyone in your life with whom God might want you to share your faith?

If so, what steps could you take this week to begin this process?

Signs of Grace

Romans 11:1-12

I ask, then, has God rejected his people? By no means! I myself am an Israelite, a descendant of Abraham, a member of the tribe of Benjamin....So too at the present time there is a remnant, chosen by grace. But if it is by grace, it is no longer on the basis of works, otherwise grace would no longer be grace.

(Romans 11:1, 5-6, NRSV)

...Not Ashamed of the Gospel

God's grace is always at work, but sometimes we have to look closely to see it. By stepping back and observing the big picture, we can get a clearer perspective on what God is doing. And Paul uses this chapter to do just that.

In chapters 9 and 10, Paul has painted the Israelites as a pretty stubborn people. They are misguided, disobedient, and hardened. It appears as though God has given up on them, and we can understand why. After all, they have rejected God's plan.

But amazingly, God has not rejected them. Paul himself is a sign that God's plan continues to include the people of Israel. Paul's miraculous conversion shows that even the most misguided, stubborn people are not without hope. They too can still be brought back. The Lord is willing to go to great lengths to try to reach them.

But there is a second sign of God's grace to the Israelites. The fact that God chose Paul, a devout Jew, to bring the gospel to the Gentiles, shows us that the Jews are still being used to accomplish God's purposes. So God's grace not only continues to be extended *to* the Jews, it is extended *through* the Jews. We see that grace in the life of Paul, as we saw it with countless Israelites throughout the Old Testament.

...Not Ashamed of Digging Deeper

Paul is the sign that God is not finished with the Chosen People. They are still close to God's heart, even though many of them are unresponsive. God will continue to pursue them.

So when it comes to God's plan, we should be careful not

to close the book too soon. Because God's plan isn't finished till the last chapter is through. This is not only true for the Jewish people of Paul's day, it's true in our lives too.

1. What does this passage show you about God's plan for salvation?

2. Have you ever experienced God working in your life through something that looked bad but turned out good?

3. How can you look for signs of God's grace in a situation you face right now? Who or what could help you see it?

Love's Secret Strategy

Romans 11:13-24

Now I am speaking to you Gentiles. Inasmuch then as I am an apostle to the Gentiles, I glorify my ministry in order to make my own people jealous and thus save some of them. For if their rejection is the reconciliation of the world, what will their acceptance be but life from the dead! ...

...Not Ashamed of the Gospel

Note then the kindness and the severity of God: severity toward those who have fallen, but God's kindness toward you, provided you continue in his kindness; otherwise you also will be cut off. And even those of Israel, if they do not persist in unbelief, will be grafted in, for God has the power to graft them in again. (Romans 11:13-15, 22-23, NRSV)

Here is a lesson about love you don't want to miss. If you love someone, and he or she doesn't love you back, there is one thing you can do to get his or her attention: start loving someone else. I know it sounds weird, but it's true. Something about our human nature causes us to want something more when someone else has it. That's a secret strategy concerning love.

However there is a slight drawback to this plan. If it works, and the person you love starts loving you, you'll now have two people to love. And that can be a big problem—unless, of course, you are God.

In this passage, we learn that God is familiar with this strategy and uses it in winning the Jews' love. By offering salvation to the Gentiles, God's love has been widened to include more than just the Jews. But unlike us, God is big enough to handle it. It is clear from this passage that God still loves the Jews. Now God's love is also directed toward the Gentiles. But this isn't a problem for God. There is enough room in God's love for both!

...Not Ashamed of Digging Deeper

Those of us who are Gentiles should be happy about this passage. By giving us a chance to be "grafted" into the tree of life, God has extended salvation to us. But God has not forgotten the Jews. God loves them, and longs for their branches to be reattached by accepting Christ and living by faith. And we learn from this passage that God's tree of life can accommodate both the Jews and the Gentiles.

Paul hopes that God's love for the Gentiles will make the Jews jealous enough to want God back. He knows that's love's secret strategy. But the good news is that the Gentiles won't be cut off if this happens. Because when God uses this strategy, there's room enough for us all.

1. Have you ever experienced the feeling of wanting something more because someone else had it?

How is that similar to God's strategy with the Jews?

2. What does God's process with the Jews show you about the way God works?

Have you ever experienced God working a similar way in your own life? When?

3. How might God use the love the two of you share to cause someone in your life to want God's love too?

The Big Picture

Romans 11:25-36

Oh, the depth of the riches of the wisdom and knowledge of God! How unsearchable his judgments, and his paths beyond tracing out! "Who has known the mind of the Lord? Or who has been his counselor?" "Who has ever given to God, that God should repay him?" For from him and through him and to him are all things. To him be the glory forever! Amen.
(Romans 11:33-36, NIV)

...Not Ashamed of the Gospel

My mom was into needlepoint. She used to buy sewing mats with pictures on them and needlepoint the picture that was on the mat. I can remember looking at the needlepoint before it was done; and since she worked from the back side, it looked like a mess. But after she finished, she'd turn the needlepoint over and I was always amazed at what I saw.

In this passage, Paul has a similar experience as he steps back and looks at God's plan. For the last three chapters, he's been talking about the Israelites being cut off, and Gentiles being grafted in. The description of what God has been doing is similar to the back side of a needlepoint. But now, he stops to consider the big picture; and he is in awe of what he sees.

Paul has already stated that when the Jews rejected Christ,

God made room for the Gentiles to accept Christ. What Paul now says is that God did this for the benefit of the Jews. It was the Jews' disobedience that brought them the need to experience God's mercy. So God allowed their disobedience for the good it would bring.

...Not Ashamed of Digging Deeper

The only way we can experience mercy is when we know that we have been disobedient. Think about it. If someone said, "I forgive you," and you didn't think that you had done anything wrong, wouldn't you feel a little offended? That's how the Jews felt. When Paul said that God sent Jesus to forgive them for their sins, they didn't think that they needed forgiveness. But after they rejected God's son and became blind to God's plan, they were finally in a place to receive grace. Now all they had to do was ask.

So Paul reveals the big picture of what God has been doing. This gives us a great insight into God's plan for us. It may seem messy while it's happening; but from the other side, it's an amazing sight.

...Not Ashamed of Living for Christ

1. What does this passage show you about the way God works in our lives?

2. Do you think that God is always in control of what happens—even when it seems bad? Why?

3. Does anything in your life right now look like a mess? What?

If you stepped back and looked at that mess from a bigger perspective, would it look the same? Why?

Living Sacrifices

Romans 12:1-2

I appeal to you therefore, brothers and sisters, by the mercies of God, to present your bodies as a living sacrifice, holy and acceptable to God, which is your spiritual worship. Do not be conformed to this world, but be transformed by the renewing of your minds, so that you may discern what is the will of God—what is good and acceptable and perfect. (Romans 12:1-2, NRSV)

...Not Ashamed of the Gospel

In the Old Testament, when people came together to worship, they would offer a sacrifice to express their devotion to God. They would carefully select a mammal or bird and then bring it to the altar. They would lay their hands on the animal's head, as a symbol of identifying with the animal before it was sacrificed. This was how people received forgiveness and reaffirmed their commitment to God.

That's probably what Paul has in mind when he tells us we are to be "living sacrifices." No longer do we offer dead animal sacrifices, because Jesus' death has taken away the need. Instead, we offer *ourselves* as *living* sacrifices, because Jesus' life gives us the incentive.

So what does it mean to be a "living sacrifice"? Living in a way that honors God. Paul shows us how to do that in the next verse. He says, "Do not be conformed to this world, but be transformed by the renewing of your minds" (verse 2). In other words, we are supposed to influence the world, rather than to be influenced by it.

...Not Ashamed of Digging Deeper

One way to think about it is to consider the difference between a thermostat and a thermometer. A thermostat sets the temperature in the room. A thermometer takes the temperature in the room. As living sacrifices, we're supposed to be thermostats instead of thermometers.

Christians are supposed to make a difference. The temperature is changed by a thermostat, and the world is changed by people who live for God. That's what it means to be a living sacrifice. And that is what you and I are called to be.

1. How does our being a living sacrifice compare with the sacrifices people gave in the Old Testament?

...Not Ashamed of Living for Christ

What similarities do you see? What differences?

2. Would you consider yourself a living sacrifice? How?

Are there any areas of your life where you are not a living sacrifice?

3. Would you describe your Christian life as a thermostat or a thermometer? Why?

The Body of Christ

Romans 12:3-8

For as in one body we have many members, and not all the members have the same function, so we, who are many, are one body in Christ, and individually we are members one of another. We have gifts that differ according to the grace given us: prophecy, in proportion to faith; ministry, in ministering; the teacher, in teaching; the exhorter, in exhortation; the giver, in generosity; the leader, in diligence; the compassionate, in cheerfulness.
(Romans 12:4-8, NRSV)

...Not Ashamed of the Gospel

God has given you a gift. But it's not for you to keep. It is for you to use. When you became a Christian, God made you part of the body of Christ. And your gift tells you what body part you are.

If serving is your gift, you might be a hand. If you have insight about people, you're probably an eye. If you like helping people learn, you could be a brain. If you're a good listener, you might be an ear. And if you like encouraging people, you could be a heart. So if you had to describe yourself as a body part, which part would it be?

If you decided not to use your gift, what would the Body look like? If your gift was serving and you didn't serve, there would be no hand. If you had the gift of teaching and you didn't teach, there would be no brain. In a very real sense, the

Body is whole or not whole because of you. Doesn't that make you feel important?

On the other hand, you're not so important that you can run the body all by yourself. Imagine if you were an eye and you felt that you didn't need any other body parts. You would look like Billy Crystal's character in *Monsters, Inc.* We're not supposed to be a giant eye or a giant ear. We are supposed to be the Body. So the more we humbly do our part, the more healthy the Body will be.

...Not Ashamed of Digging Deeper

As Christians, we need our body to be healthy so that others will look our way. If we are out of shape, the world will overlook us. But if we are in shape, the world will take notice. Chances are that if they do, others want what we have. And our body will continue to grow.

That's why it's so important to do our part. It's the way we minister to one another. But it's also the way we can witness to the world.

1. If you had to describe yourself as a body part, which part would you be? Why?

...Not Ashamed of Living for Christ

2. If you know what body part you are, how are you using your gifts for God? If you don't know, who knows you well enough to help you figure it out?

3. Would you say that you are doing a good job using your gifts? In what ways?

If not, how could you use them more effectively?

The Meaning of Love

Romans 12:9-16

Love must be sincere. Hate what is evil; cling to what is good. Be devoted to one another in brotherly love. Honor one another above yourselves. Never be lacking in zeal, but keep your spiritual fervor, serving the Lord. Be joyful in hope, patient in affliction, faithful in prayer. Share with God's people who are in need. Practice hospitality. (Romans 12:9-13, NIV)

...Not Ashamed of the Gospel

According to this passage, love is not something you feel—it's something you do. That is a very different view of love. In our world, love is sung about, written about, and acted out in ways that make us believe that it is an overwhelming emotion. When you feel it, it compels you to act. But what happens when you stop *feeling* it?

When you first fall in love, you are willing to do anything for that person. You listen to problems, do homework together, exchange little gifts. Sooner or later, the excitement fades; and you find yourself doing less and less to act on your love. But the reality is, you weren't acting on love to begin with. You were acting on feelings.

That's completely different from the love Paul describes in this passage. The love he describes is not based on feelings. It's based on actions. He doesn't say, "Love when you feel sincere." That would be easy. He says, "Love *must* be sincere—whether you feel like being sincere or not." He doesn't say, "Be devoted in romantic love." He says, "Be devoted in *brotherly* love." He doesn't use verbs like *feel, want,* and *desire.* He uses verbs like *cling, honor,* and *share.*

...Not Ashamed of Digging Deeper

To Paul, love is not a feeling. We don't love first and then act. We act first, and then love. The surprising thing is that the more we act, the more we love; and the feelings eventually come. But we're not *dependent* on those feelings, so we can be much more consistent in our love.

That is the kind of love we are to have for one another, because it's a reflection of the love God has for us.

1. Which have you experienced more in your life—a love based on feelings or a love based on actions?

2. Is there anyone in your life you love even when you don't feel like it?

How is this different from a love driven by feelings?

Is it stronger or weaker?

3. Why do you think God wants us to love by our actions rather than our feelings?

What relationship in your life do you need to show more love by your actions?

How to Conquer Evil

Romans 12:17-21

Do not repay anyone evil for evil. Be careful to do what is right in the eyes of everybody. If it is possible, as far as it depends on you, live at peace with everyone.... On the contrary: "If your enemy is hungry, feed him; if he is thirsty, give him something to drink. In doing this, you will heap burning coals on his head." Do not be overcome by evil, but overcome evil with good.
(Romans 12:17-18, 20-21, NIV)

...Not

Ashamed

of the Gospel

If you want to drive your enemies crazy, here's a tip: Love them. They won't know what hit them. They are counting on your anger. They want your revenge. They need your negativity to fuel their hatred. So your love will really throw them off. And they'll be left fighting with no one but themselves.

I know—it's easier said than done. It's hard to love someone you don't even like. The funny thing is, just as we learned in the last passage, once you start acting on love, you actually start feeling love. And there is no way to explain it until you try.

You may not be ready to love the person, but you can start by not hating him or her. Prayer really helps. It is hard to pray for someone and hate that person at the same time. Once you bring God into a

relationship, anger and bitterness start melting away; because God's love can do what your love can't. And you can rely on that love to help you.

Some enemies have done things that seem impossible to forgive. That's why Paul says to leave your revenge with the Lord. God will deal with sin—we can be assured of that. But our heart is not helped if we allow other people's sin to dominate our thoughts.

...Not

Ashamed

of Digging

Deeper

The only person who really gets hurt by your bitterness is you. That's why God wants you to release it. God's desire is for you to be free. And the only way you can experience this freedom is by letting go of your anger and pain.

The strange thing is, once you take a step to change, often your enemy changes too. You end up winning him or her over by your love. So the next time you want to beat your enemy, do it with love. It's the most effective strategy of all.

1. Who is the hardest person in your life to love?

Why is it so hard to love him or her?

2. Have you ever taken the first step toward mending a relationship—even when you didn't feel like it? If so, what was it like?

3. Is there someone in your life you know that God is calling you to love? Who?

What can you do this week to start taking a step in that direction?

Respect for Authority

Romans 13:1-7

Let every person be subject to the governing authorities; for there is no authority except from God, and those authorities that exist have been instituted by God. Therefore whoever resists authority resists what God has appointed, and those who resist will incur judgment.... Pay to all what is due them—taxes to whom taxes are due, revenue to whom revenue is due, respect to whom respect is due, honor to whom honor is due. (Romans 13:1-2, 7, NRSV)

...Not Ashamed of the Gospel

I love to drive with my fiancé, Brian, onto the Marine base at Camp Pendleton. He is a colonel; so he has a special sticker on his car, and people salute us as we approach the gate. When we walk around the Base, the other Marines address him as "Sir." That is, unless we happen to run into a general. Then Brian is the one who says "Sir."

One thing I've learned about the Marine Corps is that they know how to respect authority. Paul says in this passage that Christians should do the same. If people are in authority above you, you are to respect them— whether they are parents, teachers, or government officials. In doing so, you will be respecting the sovereignty of God.

But what if the person in authority is difficult for you to respect? That's when you can learn from the Marines. When they salute a person in a car because of a sticker, they are showing respect to the office that sticker represents. The Marines don't even know who's in the car. That's why I get saluted— not because of who I am, but because of whose car I'm in. (As much as I'd like to believe otherwise). And this a great distinction for us to understand as Christians.

...Not Ashamed of Digging Deeper

When people are in positions of authority, we are called to respect their office. But what they do with their authority will determine whether we respect them as people. Nevertheless, Paul says that we are called to respect their position. We are to give them the respect their office deserves.

So the next time you're having trouble respecting someone's authority, think of the Marines. And consider yourself lucky. You probably don't have to salute.

...Not Ashamed of Living for Christ

1. Do you have trouble respecting authority? (Think of the way you treat parents, teachers, and so forth.) If so, how can this passage help you with that?

2. Is there someone in a position of authority you have a difficult time respecting? If so, why?

How can you use the lessons of this passage to help you respect him or her?

3. What is the difference in respecting a person in authority and respecting a person's position of authority?

Can you do one without the other?

Do you need to learn to respect someone in your life now?

The Debt We Can't Pay Off

Romans 13:8-10

Owe no one anything, except to love one another; for the one who loves another has fulfilled the law. The commandments, "You shall not commit adultery; You shall not murder; You shall not steal; You shall not covet"; and any other commandment, are summed up in this word, "Love your neighbor as yourself." Love does no wrong to a neighbor; therefore, love is the fulfilling of the law. (Romans 13:8-10, NRSV)

...Not Ashamed of the Gospel

Have you ever been in debt? It's no fun. Every time you earn some money, you know that the money is not really yours. It belongs to someone else. That's why you want to pay off your debt as soon as possible.

But what if you had a debt you could never pay off? Then everything you earned would belong to someone else. That would be a drag—unless that someone happened to be God.

According to Paul, there is one debt we owe God that we can never pay off: the debt to love. But the good news is, that debt cancels out the rest. Paul lists our other debts in the form of commandments in verse 9, "You shall not commit adultery, you shall not murder, you shall not steal, you shall covet." You could try to pay each of these debts individually by focusing on what *not* to do. Or

you could pay them all at once by focusing on what *to* do: "love your neighbor as yourself".

When we love one another, we automatically fulfill the commandments of how to treat one another. That's how we pay off those debts.

...Not Ashamed of Digging Deeper

But our debt to love never ends. God wants us to pay on that debt for the rest of our lives.

Unlike other debts that hold us captive, this is one debt that sets us free. Other debts we have to pay ourselves. But the resources for this debt are found in God's love. All we have to do is draw from that Source to fill our bank accounts—and we have enough there to make payments for the rest of our lives.

Paul says that this is one debt we will never be able to pay off. But that doesn't mean we shouldn't die trying.

1. Have you ever been in debt? If so, how did it feel?

...Not Ashamed of Living for Christ

2. How does loving our neighbor fulfill all the commandments?

Is it really that simple, or do we have to do more?

3. Is there a "neighbor" you are not loving, based on your actions? If so, what could you do to love him or her better?

How can God's love help you love him or her better?

Dressing the Part

Romans 13:11-14

Let us then lay aside the works of darkness and put on the armor of light; let us live honorably as in the day, not in reveling and drunkenness, not in debauchery and licentiousness, not in quarreling and jealousy. Instead, put on the Lord Jesus Christ, and make no provision for the flesh, to gratify its desires.
(Romans 13:12b-14, NRSV)

...Not Ashamed of the Gospel

One of the best parts about being in a play is when you have your first dress rehearsal. Somehow, when you put on that costume, you feel so much more like the character you are trying to portray. There is something about dressing the part that transforms you. That is exactly the point Paul is trying to make in this passage.

When he says ,"Put on the Lord Jesus Christ," (verse 14) Paul is telling us to *dress* the part so that we can *live* the part. As Christians, we are the representatives of Christ. If we take the time to clothe ourselves with his presence, we'll be more likely to live like him in this world. Like a play, our earthly lives are limited. And one day, the curtain will go down. When that happens, we will be with Jesus forever. But until then,

we are called to live like Jesus—and it helps if we dress the part.

How do we "dress like Jesus?" It's more of an inward costume change than an outward one. Paul gives us the clothes we need in this passage.

He says that we are to "put on the armor of light" (verse 12). When we do that, our private habits and sins are revealed. These are the things we need to "take off" or put aside in order to clothe ourselves with Christ. In a play, you have to take off your own clothes to put on the clothes of your character. As Christians, we have to do the same. By putting on the armor

...Not Ashamed of Digging Deeper

of light, you can see what you need to get rid of to make room for the clothes of Christ.

Like being in a play, there will be times when you feel more into character and times when you don't. But if you make the effort to "dress like Jesus" on the inside, you will be more motivated to act like Jesus on the outside. Try it and see.

1. What do you think Paul means when he says, "Put on the armor of light"?

...Not Ashamed of Living for Christ

What would that mean for you?

2. What things do you need to "take off" in order to clothe yourself with Christ? (Think about any attitudes or sins that stand in the way.)

3. Would people identify you as a Christian by the way you act? If not, what needs to change so that they will?

Freedom to Choose

Romans 14:1-9

Welcome those who are weak in faith, but not for the purpose of quarreling over opinions. Some believe in eating anything, while the weak eat only vegetables. Those who eat must not despise those who abstain, and those who abstain must not pass judgment on those who eat; for God has welcomed them. Who are you to pass judgment on servants of another? It is before their own lord that they stand or fall. And they will be upheld, for the Lord is able to make them stand. (Romans 14:1-4, NRSV)

...Not Ashamed of the Gospel

I don't eat red meat. It's not that I'm against it. I just don't care to eat it. But I'm not a vegetarian, because I do eat chicken and turkey. Vegetarians don't eat any meat at all. They get their protein from fish, cheese, and eggs. But there are some vegetarians that don't eat any animal products at all. They eat only grains, fruits, and vegetables.

So the next time you use the term *vegetarian*, remember that there are quite a few types, depending on dietary convictions. And the next time you use the term *Christian*, it would be good to remember the same thing. This passage explains why.

Paul says that there are many kinds of Christians, with different kinds of faith. And God accepts them all. If they have faith in Jesus Christ as their Lord and Savior, they are all considered Christians. They just have different ways of expressing their faith. That's what makes the Body of Christ so interesting.

If you've ever been to a multi-denominational event, you've seen that. Some people quietly close their eyes and pray. Others lift their hands and shout. Some Christians dress a certain way, while others dress whatever way they want. Some Christians love to dance. Others don't feel that dancing is appropriate. Some think that it's OK to have a glass of wine with dinner. Others feel funny about that, so they stay away from alcohol in any form. None of these things are right or wrong—they are just

...Not Ashamed of Digging Deeper

preferences. It's important to understand the difference between precepts and preferences.

Precepts are God's commands, and all of us are supposed to obey those commands. Preferences are choices you and I have within those commands. What Paul is saying here is that we need to respect one another's preferences.

So the next time you see a Christian doing something you don't do, don't assume that it's wrong. It may just be different. And it could help you discover something new about God.

1. What are some of the preferences Paul lists in this passage?

...Not Ashamed of Living for Christ

What are some different preferences you've seen in the lives of people around you?

2. Have you ever been with a Christian who had different convictions (or preferences) than you? How did it make you feel?

3. How can you tell the difference between a personal conviction and a command from God? Why is this important?

Judging Others

Romans 14:10-13

Why do you pass judgment on your brother or sister? Or you, why do you despise your brother or sister? For we will all stand before the judgment seat of God. For it is written, "As I live, says the Lord, every knee shall bow to me, and every tongue shall give praise to God." So then, each of us will be accountable to God.

...Not Ashamed of the Gospel

Let us therefore no longer pass judgment on one another, but resolve instead never to put a stumbling block or hindrance in the way of another. (Romans 14:10-13, NRSV)

Have you ever eaten meat while dining with a vegetarian? If so, you know that there are two possible experiences. You can be with someone who will quietly order a non-meat entrée and not say a word. But there are those vegetarians who will watch you order a steak or a lamb chop and stare at your food disapprovingly. They may even softly hum "Mary had a little lamb." By the time you leave the table, you'll feel as if you had committed a crime. And you probably won't have dinner with him or her any time soon.

In this passage, Paul says that we are supposed to live our convictions without judgment. Unfortunately, Christians can be some of the most judgmental people in the world. This is ironic, since the gospel message rests entirely on grace. We represent the gospel best when we allow people the freedom to respond to God's convictions, instead of pressuring them to follow ours.

Being judgmental doesn't work, anyway. When you look down on someone, it makes him or her want to rebel. So judgment actually has the opposite effect of what you're trying to accomplish. Eventually, people start avoiding you. And that's not a great way to draw people to Christ.

...Not Ashamed of Digging Deeper

It is appropriate to help other Christians live out their convictions. But wait until they ask. Until then, live your own convictions quietly and strongly in their presence. You will be amazed at how effective your silent witness can be.

So the next time you decide not to order mahi mahi because you're trying to save the dolphins, resist the temptation to hum the theme song to *Flipper*. That will give people the freedom to live their own convictions, instead of being pressured to follow yours.

1. Have you ever encountered a really judgmental person? How did it make you feel?

...Not Ashamed of Living for Christ

2. Why does this passage say that we are not to be judgmental?

How does not being judgmental leave room for God to work?

3. On a scale of 1–10 (with 1 being nonjudgmental and 10 being very judgmental), how judgmental are you? What words in this passage speak most directly to you?

Support Where It Counts

Romans 14:14-23

I know and am persuaded in the Lord Jesus that nothing is unclean in itself; but it is unclean for anyone who thinks it unclean. If your brother or sister is being injured by what you eat, you are no longer walking in love. Do not let what you eat cause the ruin of one for whom Christ died. So do not let your good be spoken of as evil. For the kingdom of God is not food and drink but righteousness and peace and joy in the Holy Spirit. The one who thus serves Christ is acceptable to God and has human approval. (Romans 14:14-18, NRSV)

...Not Ashamed of the Gospel

Have you ever spent a day with a friend who is trying to lose weight? Sometimes it is a challenge to be supportive. Especially when you are really hungry. Without noticing it, you start saying things like, "Gosh, a pizza sounds really good," or "I really feel like some ice cream." Suddenly, the carrots you two are munching on just aren't cutting it; and your friend suggests calling Dominoes.

Now you've got a choice. Your friend has been miserable because she wants to lose weight. But she's ready to throw her diet out the door to eat pizza with you. You feel a twinge of guilt because you know that she'll regret it. But your mouth is already watering for that pepperoni pizza. What should you do?

According to this passage, you should skip the pizza and support your friend. Because you can eat pizza later, when she isn't around. This is a time when you can come alongside your friend in an area where she is weak. And she'll thank you for it when she steps on the scale.

...Not Ashamed of Digging Deeper

Paul says that we are to do everything we can to keep from causing our brothers or sisters to stumble. That means sacrificing our own freedom for the sake of their well-being. If you don't need to be on a diet, but your friend does, choosing to eat carrots instead of pizza is something you're doing for her—not yourself. That is one small way you can reflect the presence of Christ.

When you exercise this discipline, you can draw on the

strength of Jesus to do it. After all, he was God, but he became a man *for us*. He endured poverty, shame, and criticism *for us*. He had nails driven in his hands *for us*. And he suffocated on a cross *for us*.

Suddenly, skipping pizza doesn't seem that hard after all.

...Not Ashamed of Living for Christ

1. Have you ever supported a friend by making a sacrifice in your own life? Has anyone ever done that for you?

2. Why does God want us to help one another when we are weak?

3. Is there a specific friend or family member who you know is struggling with something? How can you show support to him or her right now?

The Strong and the Weak

Romans 15:1-4

We who are strong ought to bear with the failings of the weak and not to please ourselves. Each of us should please his neighbor for his good, to build him up. For even Christ did not please himself but, as it is written: "The insults of those who insult you have fallen on me." For everything that was written in the past was written to teach us, so that through endurance and the encouragement of the Scriptures we might have hope. (Romans 15:1-4, NIV)

...Not Ashamed of the Gospel

The movie *The Mighty* is about two boys who become best friends. One was brilliant, but he was crippled and very short. His nickname was "Freak." The other was not very smart, but he was big and strong. His nickname was "Max." It wasn't long before the two outcasts found each other and formed a bond of friendship.

On the Fourth of July, the two friends went together to a carnival to watch the fireworks. As they moved into the crowd to watch the display, Freak started shouting, "Down in front!" He was too short to see above the crowd. Suddenly, Max reached down and put him on his shoulders; and Freak was able to see fireworks for the very first time.

From that point forward, the two boys stayed together. With Freak on top of Max's shoulders as the head and Max on the bottom as the body, they were able to draw from each other's strengths, and compensate for each other's weaknesses. And they referred to themselves as "The Mighty." Together they could accomplish what neither of them could do alone.

...Not Ashamed of Digging Deeper

Paul says, "We who are strong ought to bear with the failings of the weak" (verse 1). There will be times when we will be both. We are strong in some areas and weak in others. So we are supposed to use our strengths to help others in their weakness, and draw from their strengths to help us in our own times of weakness. This is what brings unity to the Body of Christ.

Some of us need to work on lending our strengths to others. Others of us need to work on accepting others' strengths to compensate for our own. Both take a spirit of humility and grace. But as Paul says in verse 3, we can draw from Christ's example to accomplish it.

So we can be alone and weak or together and mighty—the choice is up to us.

1. Do you think that Christians are separated into two categories—weak and strong? Or do you think that Christians are all weak *and* strong? Why?

...Not Ashamed of Living for Christ

2. In what areas are you strong? In what areas are you weak?

3. Why do you think God wants us to lean on one another for strength?

Do you have a hard time leaning on others? Why?

All for One, One for All

Romans 15:5-12

May the God who gives endurance and encouragement give you a spirit of unity among yourselves as you follow Christ Jesus, so that with one heart and mouth you may glorify the God and Father of our Lord Jesus Christ.

Accept one another, then, just as Christ accepted you, in order to bring praise to God. (Romans 15:5-7, NIV)

...Not Ashamed of the Gospel

One Sunday, while I was a youth pastor in Berkeley, California, our congregation was taking Communion, when I suddenly had the biggest urge to laugh. (Has that ever happened to you?) It wasn't appropriate during Communion, but it just struck me how diverse our congregation was. There was Rick, who was blind, standing behind Vivian, who was really short. Across the room, Melvin, who was a doctor, stood next to Doug, our church janitor. Ralph, a retired Navy commander, was in the balcony with Octavian, a Romanian engineer. Liberal Democrats sat next to conservative Republicans. Different races sat together in the same pews. Children held hands with grandparents. And the reason all of these people were there was because of Jesus Christ.

That is the picture I think of when I think of the ideal church. And that's the picture Paul describes in this passage. In verse 7, he says that our unity and acceptance of one another brings praise to God—and it's true. When an extremely diverse group of individuals come together, it shows that there must be something powerful that unifies them. What a testimony to the power of God!

...Not Ashamed of Digging Deeper

"All for one, and one for all." This phrase from the *Three Musketeers* is a great theme for this passage. We come together in the church for One—Jesus Christ. And Jesus is there for us all.

That's what I experienced that day during Communion, and I have never forgotten it. Because when I looked around and saw the diversity of those faces, I think that what I was really looking at was the face of Jesus Christ.

...Not Ashamed of Living for Christ

1. What is the best example you have seen of unity among Christians?

What is the best experience you have had being unified with other Christians?

2. Is it necessary to be accepting of others in order to be unified with them? Why?

3. Has it ever been difficult for you to be unified with another Christian? If so, how did you handle it?

How would you handle it differently after reading this passage?

Hope and Power

May the God of hope fill you with all joy and peace in believing, so that you may abound in hope by the power of the Holy Spirit.

I myself feel confident about you, my brothers and sisters, that you yourselves are full of goodness, filled with all knowledge, and able to instruct one another. Nevertheless on some points I have written to you rather boldly by way of reminder, because of the grace given me by God.

(Romans 15:13-15, NRSV)

...Not

Ashamed

of the Gospel

I am having a God moment right now. Have you ever had one of those? You're sitting there, minding your own business when all of a sudden God speaks to you. It's not an audible voice (that hasn't happened to me yet), but you know that it's God. While I was writing this devotional, Romans 15:13 popped out of my Bible and grabbed me. So I decided that God wanted me to tell you about it.

I'm going through a scary time right now. I'm getting married, and God is allowing some of my insecurities to be exposed—and I'm afraid. Then I sit down to write this devotional for *you*, and God uses this devotional to minister to *me*. That is what is so cool about God. We can be ministered to at any time—even when we're ministering to

others! Maybe especially when we're ministering to others.

When Paul speaks about his ministry to the Gentiles, he says that it was his own experience with God that gave him the grace and power to minister to them. That's how it is for us.

...Not
Ashamed
of Digging
Deeper

When we experience God's power in our own life, we are more passionate about sharing it with others. And our lives, not just our words, become our witness.

That is my story right now. God used this verse to fill me with hope, because I can trust the power of the Holy Spirit. That will help me overcome my fears. And you know what? I'm experiencing the peace of this promise right now.

So that's what God wanted me to share with you. I hope that it will encourage you to share your life story with others. Paul did, and the world was changed because of it.

I wonder what God could do through you?

1. Is there an area of your life right now where you need to experience hope?

How can the words in this passage help you?

2. Have you ever taken the risk to share with someone else what God is doing in your life? If so, what happened? If not, what has kept you from doing so?

3. Think of one thing God is doing in your life right now (teaching you, convicting you, or challenging you). Write the name of one person you could share this with this week.

God's Purpose for Your Life

Romans 15:20-33

It has always been my ambition to preach the gospel where Christ was not known, so that I would not be building on someone else's foundation. Rather, as it is written:

"Those who were not told about him will see, and those who have not heard will understand." This is why I have often been hindered from coming to you.

...Not Ashamed of the Gospel

But now that there is no more place for me to work in these regions, and since I have been longing for many years to see you, I plan to do so when I go to Spain. I hope to visit you while passing through and to have you assist me on my journey there, after I have enjoyed your company for a while.

(Romans 15:20-24, NIV)

What is God's purpose for your life? Do you know? Paul shares his in this passage. Maybe the way he shares his purpose will help you discover yours.

In verse 20, Paul says, "It has always been my ambition to preach the gospel where Christ was not known." That's Paul's call. Frederick Buechner (one of my favorite authors) once said that your purpose from God is where your greatest passion meets the world's greatest need. That is a good way to figure it out.

Paul's greatest passion was to share Christ with others. The world's greatest need was where Christ had not yet been preached. So Paul became a missionary. This passage describes his travels. The speaking and sharing Paul did came out of his passion to share the gospel. His ministry continues today through his writings, which we have in our Bibles.

How blessed we are that Paul followed God's call. How blessed others will be if we do the same! God created you for a purpose. You are the only

...Not Ashamed of Digging Deeper

you there ever was or ever will be. If you don't live out your purpose, what a loss for the rest of us! When I get to the end of my life, God will not say to me, "Laurie, why weren't you Moses?" But what a tragedy if God said to me, "Laurie, why weren't you Laurie?"

So I ask you again, what is God's purpose for your life? The fact that you're reading this devotion shows that you are interested in finding out. Don't get hung up on God's plan for your future. Just seek God right now, where you are; and you will be shown your purpose for today. It will be what you want to do—and what your world needs most from you.

If you start living your days this way, your purpose will unfold. You'll see.

1. How do you see Paul's purpose fulfilled in this passage?

...Not Ashamed of Living for Christ

How do you see his purpose fulfilled throughout the New Testament?

2. If someone asked you, "What's your purpose in life?" what would you say?

3. Where does your greatest passion meet the world's greatest need?

If you don't know, who could help you discover it? If you do know, what could you do this week to start living it out?

Friends in Christ

Romans 16:1-16

I commend to you our sister Phoebe, a servant of the church in Cenchrea. I ask you to receive her in the Lord in a way worthy of the saints and to give her any help she may need from you, for she has been a great help to many people, including me.

...Not Ashamed of the Gospel

Greet Priscilla and Aquila, my fellow workers in Christ Jesus. They risked their lives for me. Not only I but all the churches of the Gentiles are grateful to them. Greet also the church that meets at their house. Greet my dear friend Epenetus, who was the first convert to Christ in the province of Asia.... Greet one another with a holy kiss. All the churches of Christ send greetings. (Romans 16:1-5, 16, NIV)

I love reading in this passage about Paul's friends. It makes me appreciate the friends God has given me. Sometimes it's good to take a moment and, like Paul, write down what you appreciate about your friends. Here are some things I appreciate about mine:

Donna and Stacy are two friends who have stood by me, laughed with me, cried with me, and prayed for me. They have truly helped shape me into the person I've become.

John, my close friend since high school, has deeply encouraged me with his growing faith in the Lord. And his great sense of humor has made me laugh for twenty years.

Vivian has been a "mom" friend who has mentored me and gently pushed me closer to Jesus.

Ramona and Synicka are two daughters in the Lord who have helped me learn what it means to be a mom before I have children of my own.

Al has gone to be with Jesus. But he was a "dad" when I needed one most.

There is also Marlo, who has shown me what it means to serve the Lord in the midst of all circumstances.

...Not Ashamed of Digging Deeper

Krista helped me learn the delicate touch of ministering to inner-city kids.

And Helen helped me look within myself during a tremendous trial and hear God's voice.

Finally, there's Brian, the true companion God has given me to share life, share burdens, and learn what love really means.

These are some friends God has used to bless my life. Why not take a moment to write down some of yours? It will help you remember how many people love you. And their presence in your life will show how much you are loved by God.

1. What are some of the things Paul appreciates in his friends?

...Not Ashamed of Living for Christ

What do you appreciate in a good friend?

2. Why is it important to appreciate our friends?

How does your appreciation encourage them?

How does theirs encourage us?

3. Take a moment and write the names of five to ten friends God has given you and what you appreciate about them. Consider dropping them a line to let them know.

Final Words

Romans 16:17-27

I urge you, brothers [and sisters], to watch out for those who cause divisions and put obstacles in your way that are contrary to the teaching you have learned. Keep away from them. For such people are not serving our Lord Christ, but their own appetites. By smooth talk and flattery they deceive the minds of naive people....

...Not Ashamed of the Gospel

Now to him who is able to establish you by my gospel and the proclamation of Jesus Christ, according to the revelation of the mystery hidden for long ages past, but now revealed and made known through the prophetic writings by the command of the eternal God, so that all nations might believe and obey him—to the only wise God be glory forever through Jesus Christ! Amen.
(Romans 16:17-18, 25-27, NIV)

Now Paul is ready to sign off, but he has some final words to say before he's through. So listen up.

The first thing he says is to be wise about the company you keep. That is good advice. Whether you like it or not, you are influenced by the people around you. Have you noticed when two people become friends, they start dressing alike, talking alike, and using the same mannerisms? The same thing probably happens to you. It's not that you try to do it, you just do. It is something that happens as you spend time together.

That's why people get into trouble when they pick the wrong friends. Paul says that in verse 17. He knows that the more you hang out with the wrong crowd, the more you'll be influenced by them. And he wants you to stand firm with what you know is right.

It's not that you can't be friends with people who aren't Christians. You just need to be wise about who is influencing who. Think for a moment. If you have some friends who are not Christians, would you say you have a bigger influence on them, or

...Not Ashamed of Diggin Deeper

that they have a bigger influence on you? Sometimes you have to be honest with yourself to see the truth.

The other piece of advice Paul gives is to be wise about what is good and to be innocent about what is evil. We live in a culture that does the exact opposite. It's challenging to do the right thing when we are surrounded by people doing the wrong thing. But we must hold to what we know is true.

In the end, truth will win out. And God can help us hold on to the truth when we feel discouraged or all alone. So, rest in those Mighty Hands. They are the Hands that will ultimately crush evil. And they are the Hands that will lead you home.

1. If you were writing final words to encourage your Christian friends to keep living the faith, what would you write?

 ...Not Ashamed of Living for Christ

2. Why do you think Paul warns the Romans (and us) to stay away from people who cause dissension and put obstacles in our way?

Is there anyone in your life like that?

3. How can you remind yourself that God is at work establishing you for the Kingdom?

Consider asking yourself two questions every day:

a. Where have I felt God's presence most?
b. Where have I felt God's presence least?

Then stay close to God.